Home Grown Kids

A
Practical Handbook
for Teaching Your
Children at Home

Raymond & Dorothy Moore

Other books by Raymond and Dorothy Moore

Better Late Than Early
School Can Wait
Home Spun Schools
Home Style Teaching
Home Built Discipline
Home Made Health
The Successful Homeschool Family Handbook (formerly Home School Burnout)
Minding Your Own Business

All available from The Moore Foundation,
Box 1, Camas, WA 98607

Home Grown Kids

A Practical Handbook for Teaching Your Children at Home

Raymond & Dorothy Moore

WORD PUBLISHING
Dallas·London·Vancouver·Melbourne

Distributed by The Moore Foundation,
Box 1, Camas, WA 98607

To mothers and fathers
who are more concerned about principle
than social pressures, who cherish
their children more than their own freedoms,
who are willing to study to provide them
sound values, academic excellence,
and a sense of self-worth

CONTENTS

FOREWORD

If there is one quality scientists seem most anxious to preserve in their research efforts, it is *objectivity*. Without it, they tend to "discover" what they had *hoped* to find, rather than valid new understandings. Nevertheless, objectivity can be extremely elusive in human endeavors. It has been my observation that all fields of science are influenced by their surrounding culture, and that investigators often produce conclusions that "miraculously" fit their own biases.

Nowhere is this lack of objectivity more evident than in behavorial research. Humanistic attitudes seem to dictate not only the outcome of many studies, but even the *topics* for investigation. Consider, for example, the research efforts that currently seem to validate the passionate views of the woman's liberation movement. Would you believe that fathers make better mothers than mothers, and that boys and girls are really not very different, and that women are less emotional than men, and that the "maternal instinct" is simply a cultural phenomenon, etc.? A review of so-called psychology articles in popular magazines will show the accommodating connection between "research" findings and the prevailing attitudes of the day.

It is this bias in behavioral research that makes me appreciate the outstanding work of Dr. Raymond Moore, whose research does not permit him to yield to the pressures of his culture. He stood like a rock during an era when developmental psychologists were universally extolling the virtues of early schooling. Indeed, the

"Great Society" programs of the sixties supplied massive federal funding for educational ventures that pulled millions of preschool boys and girls from their homes and put them in classrooms. Later, the influx of women in the labor force resulted in the proliferation of day care centers, nursery school programs and other out-of-home experiences for children. In the wake of this tidal wave of public and professional opinion, Dr. Raymond Moore confidently reported his findings: *Children suffer when taken too early from the security of their homes!*

In a world of "herd" behavior, where most of us drift along with the crowd, I'm pleased to have discovered Raymond Moore. He is one of the very few developmental psychologists in America who is deeply committed to the Christian faith, and his reverence is evident throughout his writings.

In this book, Dr. and Mrs. Moore (she, a reading specialist and church educator for children) present their conclusions about the child, the school, and the home, and provide the data to back them up. Their research and analyses as published in their many books and articles are definitive and impressive to laymen and professionals. The result is a fascinating and valuable discussion of significance to every parent. In short, this is a key book for families that care about the education of their "kids."

Dr. Moore recently appeared as a guest on my radio series, "Focus on the Family," broadcast on 200 stations. The reaction of our listeners was incredible. We received more mail in response to those programs than any we had ever aired, with better than 95 percent of the letters being highly favorable. Obviously, the Moores' perspective on early childhood education is like cool water to a parched land. It has the potential of turning the world of the preschool child into a green and lush wonderland.

I highly recommend *Home Grown Kids* to both educators and parents.

James C. Dobson, Ph.D.
Associate Clinical Professor of
Pediatrics
USC School of Medicine

A NOTE FROM THE AUTHORS

A friend and I were talking recently about a question in the Eleventh Annual Phi Delta Kappan–Gallup Poll on the Public's Attitudes Toward the Public Schools. Both of us had long been members of the fraternity and both had for years been school administrators and university professors. The question was, "Do you think that the school could help you in any way in preparing your child for school?" Fifty-three percent of the parents answered "No." And ten percent were not sure. And now many families were teaching their children at home, sometimes against the law.

"Most parents are ungrateful," he concluded.

"Why do you say that?" I asked.

"Well, Ray, just look at all the services we provide. We pick them up every morning—in many cases right from their front door—and take them to school. Every afternoon we bring them back. In between we supervise their study in the classroom or the library and their games in the gym or on the playground. We feed them a good hot lunch in the cafeteria. It's literally a public baby-sitting service," he insisted.

"But maybe that isn't what these parents need or want," I suggested. "Maybe we have been giving them the idea that they can't handle their own youngsters, and they live up to our expectations."

"Are you saying we're brainwashing them?"

"Yes, sort of. And some of them are awakening to it."

"I'm not sure if I get you."

"Which," I asked, "are harder to teach, normal children or handicapped?"

"Why, handicapped, of course."

"Does the law require them to go to school?"

"No, not generally."

"It in effect says they are all right at home with their parents?"

"Yes—with a certain amount of help."

"But they may stay home and parents are their primary teachers?"

"Yes, I guess so."

"But the law usually requires the normal child to be in school, implying that parents are not as good teachers as the school."

"Sounds like double-talk, doesn't it?"

"It is double-talk."

"Yet the state has to protect those children whose parents can't or won't meet their needs."

"Indeed, but is that the kind of parent who gave us 53 to 63 percent of the poll?"

"I see what you mean," he said.

When we make our laws and educational policies primarily for the parents who don't care, instead of for those who do, those laws are backwards. We urge that the burden of proof be on the state to show which mothers and fathers are not doing their job. And as long as parents meet the state's achievement and behavior standards, we feel they should be allowed to determine the nature of their children's education.

Certainly there are parents who are not qualified to educate their own children. But we are not speaking of those qualifications that the state often perceives, such as a teaching certificate or a college education. Rather, the unqualified parent or teacher is one whose attitude is indifferent to a youngster's real needs, or whose motives place his or her own freedoms above those of the child. We firmly believe that the greatest teaching talent in the world lies in the warm, responsive and consistent parent whose love makes the needs of his children his highest concern. If anyone disagrees, ask him for his evidence. Parents' daily one-to-one example amounts to master teaching at the highest level.

For more than forty years Dorothy and I have been puzzled about the increases in learning failure and delinquency which have come with the school pressures after World War II and especially since Sputnik in 1957. We were suspicious that psychologists were pointing us in the wrong direction and that wherever feasible children should remain longer in the home.

A combination of events, including the urgings of our son Dennis, by now a graduate student in child psychology, convinced us that more intensive research was indeed needed. Thus over a period of ten years, our private and publicly funded teams at Stanford, at the University of Colorado Medical School, and here in Michigan centered on basic research in public policy, neurophysiology, and comparative studies. We also analyzed more than 7,000 studies of young children—of their senses, reasoning, brain development, social-emotional growth, coordination, and related facets. We were forced to conclude that we should be doing more to delay schooling than to rush them in earlier. Many may have to go early to school, but most still do not. And those who delay, preferably until at least ages eight to ten should usually enter with their agemates at grades two, three, or four. The *why* of these conclusions was thoroughly documented in our book *School Can Wait*. Now we present the *how* in *Home-Grown Kids*.

There are a lot of very good nursery schools, kindergartens, and elementary schools in the world. We have visited many and administered quite a few. Yet there are none whose programs can match education by loving parents of even modest ability, working with their own children in the simplest of homes. And we must not lose this heritage and art.

The family was given to us by the same God in whom our country trusts. On the family rest the pinions of our society. Nevertheless, we have gone a long, long way toward putting it down and substituting parenting-by-state. Now leading social researchers predict the death of our democratic society within a generation. If we are to retrieve it—and our schools—we would do well to look again to God and the home.

Some parents realize this and are finding surprisingly simple answers to complex questions about the rearing of children. They are bringing new meanings to the word "family." They are rethinking the idea of mass-produced education and are coming up with the notion that maybe "custom-made" is not so elitist after all. Their youngsters are not manufactured toys; they are home-grown kids. In their children's growing process mothers and fathers are sensing more widely and deeply the purpose of the home. But few of those parents, whatever their level of education, have more than the most casual idea of their astonishing potential as educators. This is what we want them to know, along with some proven ideas of how to get the job done.

Many mothers and fathers, responding to the needs of their children and aware of their own teaching abilities, are in the vanguard of a rapidly growing home school movement. As a sequel to Home Grown Kids, we are preparing Home Spun Schools, a "how-we-did-it" book, giving the stories of a variety of highly successful home schools.

                                    Raymond S. and Dorothy Moore

Part One

THE FAMILY
OR THE STATE?

Reference numbers throughout the text of *Home Grown Kids* correspond to numbered items in the alphabetical list of References and Resources in the back of book

CHAPTER ONE

The Hand That Rocks the Cradle . . .

Going home from a day's outing, Rolf and Heidi Neumann were motoring along Robert Louis Stevenson's Silverado Trail in the upper reaches of California's lush and historic Napa Valley. Each curve of the highway brought new surprises as the pine and oak-covered mountains blended with the vineyard-strewn vale. The young couple marveled at nature's expressions, occasionally pointing to a doe in an open patch of forest or reminiscing about their honeymoon as they caught sight of a quaint cottage all but hidden in the trees. For some moments they seemed unaware of three-year-old Melanie and five-year-old Michael, playing contentedly in the rear of the station wagon. But Michael neatly took care of that. "Mommie," he interrupted, "Mommie, are we God's dream?"

"Why, yes, Mikey," Heidi responded, momentarily startled at her little boy's insights. "Why do you ask?"

"I was just wondering."

At least one pair of young ears had caught the spirit of this front seat conversation. Although nothing had been said about dreams or even about God, Mikey had drawn his own conclusions. He had identified with God and with dreams simply because his front-seat models used that kind of language.

Dorothy and I are distressed that there are any parents or educators or other very bright minds to whom such talk is foreign, especially in America, where we pledge allegiance to "one nation under God," and use currency that proclaims, "In God we Trust."

17

It distresses us also that conversation about God's reality in our lives should draw angry reactions from psychologists and scientists who insist on openness in their search for truth. No one has yet come up with a rational road around the idea of an all-wise, all-powerful God when dealing with the wonders of little children, although many have made fools of themselves trying. An overwhelming question inevitably emerges in the thoughtful parent's mind, "What really is the worth of my child?"

Five-year-old Michael without pretense reflected powerfully the values he had been taught. The parent models had clearly spoken. The Neumanns, as their names might suggest, were only two generations away from conservative European forebears whose roots gave America her divine commitment. Little wonder that Heidi and Rolf Neumann are convinced that Michael and Melanie were given them as heaven's trust.

Science and God

Their belief might still sound odd to those who are not acquainted with the Bible. Or it might appear strange to those who are not informed about the mysterious process that brings a child into the world and sees him grow. There is, for example, the growth of his brain—an amazing little watery mass of pink-grey mush, which can handle problems more complex than a computer that would cover the face of the earth. Nor could such a computer either reason or worship. Then there is the development of the eyes, each of which has more than 135,000,000 tiny receptors called "rods and cones"—which along with the other senses can bring information to the brain at a rate of 100,000,000 bits of data per second!

Any scientists who say this marvel "just happened" should, in the opinion of noted astronomer Sir James Jeans, have their own heads examined. He considered evolution's story of the "accidental" development of the universe and its human beings about as likely as the formation of an unabridged dictionary from a print shop explosion. University of California astronomers long ago pointed out that there are more worlds in the universe—not counting their suns—than there are grains of sand on the seashores of this earth. But eminent Cleveland astronomer J. J. Nassam marveled not so much at the bigness of the universe as at the mind God gave man.

It is the building of such minds in our little children that is perhaps our greatest trust from God. But why such infinite resources for such an earthy life? The Scriptures are clear that it was the original intent of God that our minds were created for eternity and that He did not plan on death for us. These writings are filled with overtones which even now suggest future lives that measure with the life of God (John 3:16, 14:1–3, etc., KJV). Paul clearly identifies us as joint heirs with the Son of God, the King of kings—if we choose Him as our King (Rom. 8:14–17, KJV). Peter repeatedly refers to our royal station (1 Pet. 2:9, KJV). And the Apostle John flatly proclaims us "kings and priests unto God" and tells precisely how and where this inheritance and coronation take place (Rev. 1:5–6; 3:20–21; 5:9–10, KJV).

So the work of parents is to share with God the making of kings! Such is the mandate from the Creator Himself, the King of all kings.

How Kings Are Made

One day during our years in Japan we hosted Senior Prince Takamatsu and his lovely princess, heiress of the legendary Tokugawa shogunate. He is a brother of Emperor Hirohito and uncle of Crown Prince Akihito. While we dined together in our home that day, the prince held our children Dennis and Kathie close by him on the sofa and told them how kings are made—how Akihito-san was being prepared for Japan's throne.

The peers of the court, he said, saw their job as a sacred responsibility. They were of course determined that the young prince would be well schooled in his studies. Yet their far greater concern was his character. His attitudes, motives, habits, manners, courtesies, way of speaking, and self-control were ever on their minds. The way he walked, the manner in which he met others, his willingness to work and to serve ranked high in their priorities. He must be educated at once in courage and patience, firmness and compassion, determination and understanding. As prince and emperor he would be an example to the Land of the Rising Sun.

He was allowed until eight or nine to remain in the warmth of his palace home, close to his father and mother, and help in the rearing of his little brother and sisters. Then he was taken a block away, each day, across the Tokyo palace moat to the Imperial Library. There, largely alone for a few years, he was taught precisely how to walk, talk, listen, react, and to have near perfect self-control under any and all circumstances.

A careful daily report of his progress was provided the emperor and empress, who warmly welcomed the princeling home at the end of each day. There was never a question about the values he was to learn. His parents and his tutors knew well that the sweetest and most poignant sociability comes not from random association with classmates, but from building a sense of self-worth and a concern for others. We later witnessed the poise of the crown prince at public and private events. He was a source of pride to the peerage and obviously of high satisfaction to his family.

Bigger is not better. If the training of a crown prince should be a sobering task for Japan's courtiers, how much more for us of common stock, who are charged with preparing kings for the throne room of God? As joint heirs with the King of kings, the heritage of our children ranks above that of an earthly monarch as the heavens are higher than the earth.

The tutorial system has never been excelled in education. And the home has been its coziest nest. Many of the great geniuses of the ages were largely schooled at home. In fact, no one has ever improved on the reasonably well-managed home school. Its only serious challenge-at-large has been the one-room rural family-type school which has been indeed a worthy complement to the home. But, for a general education, large schools have seldom proved as effective as smaller ones. Even James Bryant Conant, who fathered the "comprehensive" school for "enrichment," confessed his error before he died. Many of his enrichment centers had become educational ghettoes. Charles Evers, black mayor of Jackson, Mississippi, who once led the fight for more busing, moans the woes that bigness has brought. He says that busing—which consolidation has required—"is ridiculous." The kids "are so sleepy they can't be taught." Evers pleads for more small schools.[47]

"It's a matter of understanding what education really is," states Fran Nolan, child specialist with the State of New York. "Education isn't books and charts and tests nearly so much as it is meaningful living, and no one can provide this better than good parents." Indeed a warm, responsive, and reasonably consistent parent with little formal education can, in an hour and a half or two hours a day, easily outdistance the teacher who has twenty or thirty or more kiddies in her coop. Isn't it about time we who are teachers stop trying to convince parents that we can outparent them, and for us to sense that a teaching certificate is no guarantee of teaching skill? Rather, shouldn't we be working to turn parental feelings of inferiority into feelings of self-worth as the world's best teachers of their own children? They are particularly effective through their youngsters' value-building pre-adolescent years. They are a key to the restoration of our schools.

Some Very Heavy Costs

If our educational answers said that the more we spend on schools the better our children are educated, the home might be partly justified in its retreat. But this is not the way it is. In his now-famed report, sociologist James Coleman found that a child's success or failure in school is largely determined by the family rather than the school budget.[30, 32] Tax increases are not bringing the improvements in education that we are promised.[41] In fact, the proposals and results are far from the estimates even well-informed legislators have posed.[54] And on an intimate family basis, Cornell's Urie Bronfenbrenner found that children who spend more of their elective time with their agemates than with their parents or other family adults, have distorted views of parents, peers, and themselves.[12]

The tendency of most schools and similar institutions is to make the child's program rigid. This is a necessary feature of mass production. The youngster's activity for much of the day is focused in a few square feet of area around his desk, and timed out to the minute. As the years have rolled on, we have tightened the noose and piled on the studies, expecting the child nobly to respond with higher achievement. But it hasn't worked out that way. School records have dismally declined, with learning failure, delinquency, and hyperactivity racing for first place in HEW statistics. Is this what we want for our children?

A number of writers have pointed out the dangers of earlier and earlier institutional life for the little ones, and of the fading of old-fashioned home chores and family experience in favor of "me-first" sports and amusements.[43] But many professionals, more intent on teacher jobs and equipment sales than on the needs of children, have failed to understand that their own long-term future depends on the welfare of those in their care. If the school system fails, there may no longer be any teacher jobs as we know them now.

On the other hand, if the home is given its full share of the youngsters' time—until their learning tools are tempered and their values stabilized—the evidence is clear that it will produce far better "raw material" for the school's manufacture.[43] The home is the best possible foundation for the school. But we have weakened that base with early school entrance requirements and with curricula that cater more to indulgence than to principled character development. If during the present era of educational reassessment the state school systems do not relax their rigid control over the child's education, there is a stark prospect of wholesale rebellion. Stanford education dean J. Myron Atkin sees the possible "dismantling of universal, public, compulsory education as it has been pioneered in America."[4]

Into this smoggy educational climate the home school is bringing a breath of fresh air for many families. Parents have shown themselves to be remarkably capable tutors. Home-schooled kids have time to make things in the kitchen or garage or to go places with their parents without fear of school disruption. Their tender spirits do not have to confront the often defiling rivalry and ridicule of the classroom, playground, or bus. They make outstanding records in community leadership and service. And their parents particularly relish the privilege of teaching cherished principles and moral beliefs without pressure and without the intrusion of textbook ideas they regard as alien or amoral.

Home—The Best Early School

Many leading psychologists freely underscore the warm quality of the home. David Elkind of the University of Rochester,[18] Meredith Robinson of the Stanford Research Institute[52] and William Rohwer of California-Berkeley[53] join in suggesting that the family is the best learning nest until near adolescence—if, of course, you can provide a good home. We see that as our first and greatest educational goal—to provide good homes; homes where the children are not "burned out" by classroom pressures, as Elkind suggests; homes where warm, responsive, consistent care guarantees the most efficient education. Homes where lamblike freedom under the firm but tender nurture of the shepherd brings out learning which no school can match.

If these home schools were not doing a good job of education, the state might have reason for concern.

When several years ago the State of New York demanded that Douglas Ort put his children in school, he requested an explanation of the complaint against him. "What is really the problem?" he asked, after some discussion.

"The likely charge is 'child neglect,'" warned the well-mannered state's officer. "Usually 'criminal child neglect.'"

"It is obvious, even from your own comments," Ort reasoned, "that our children are not neglected."

"But it's the law," was the defensive retort.

"Are you," asked Ort, "more concerned about the letter of the law, a possibly bad law? Or about the real needs of our children?"

"I didn't make the laws," the man apologized, "but I must follow instructions."

"Are you worried about their achievement?" Ort inquired. "Clearly you are not concerned about their behavior."

"Well, yes, we must make sure they are up to state standards."

"What standards do you have in mind?"

"Any good standardized test, such as—"

"What is the toughest of all?"

"The Stanford Achievement battery is a good one."

"Then please test them," Ort politely challenged.

At the same time thirteen children from six home school families were tested. All achieved above the 90th percentile, or in the upper 10 percent of the nation. One of Doug Ort's children scored in the 96th percentile and the other tied with a neighbor's child in the 99th percentile. Recently, thoughtful New York school men have been patient with such home schools.

Meanwhile, in Nebraska, Lesley Sue Rice gained an average of nearly three years in one year under her high-school-educated mother. And eight-year-old Corinne Johnson of Ridgewood, New Jersey, was excelling in fifth-grade work at home.

While there are bound to be negligent parents who will encourage truancy or keep their children at home for other reasons, they should not form the basis for judgment of mothers and fathers who are truly anxious to give their children the best rearing possible, even if they have to do the teaching themselves, At The Moore Foundation, we average from dozens home school inquiries a day in our office and are frequently called for help in dealing with the law—sometimes to witness in court. Yet of all the hundreds of cases in our files, we do not know of one such home school in the nation in which the students are not performing well above average academically and behaviorally. And socially they generally excel.

Where there are problems, why not use teachers to help parents rather than to accuse all home schools? Why should home school parents have to justify their actions? Why should not the burden of proof be placed with the state? Why shouldn't the state set out first to repair the cracks in its own educational foundations, rather than searching for faults in the home school walls? *If state officials have any doubt, let them randomly visit a few family classes and compare the happy spirits with what they find in their own institutions.*

Let us then expect the state and other schools to abide by the same rigid criteria they expect of the home. For example, *there is not one state in the United States that has based its early entrance laws on systematic replicable research!*[23] On the other hand, studies have repeatedly shown that the homespun school does very well indeed, nearly always ranking well above the national averages, and some of them in the top final percent! We do not need double standards—one for the school, another for the home.

We believe that for any school district in a state to charge criminal neglect against parents who care enough for their own children to school them at home, is itself the crime, and usually against the finest of its citizens. To threaten to take away children from home when they excel mentally, socially, and morally in their home school is an astonishing miscarriage of justice in a time when there are plenty of urgent matters to occupy our courts. Yet this is precisely what has been happening from New York to California in an ostensibly godly nation.

Fortunately, these states are not without people of common sense. Recently in New York State word went out from the educational commissioner's office to be patient with home schools. California likewise has taken a far wiser and more patient course with such homes than have some other states with mandatory five- and six-year entrance laws. This tolerance is being increasingly shared from Oregon to Missouri, Mississippi, and Maryland. But the citizens of Arizona, Pennsylvania, and Washington have shown the most restraint of all. At this writing, their laws continue to require school entry no later than age eight, and they seem liberal in their interpretation.

If our public schools are to survive, we urge the state to take a positive, friendly interest in its home schools. Why not use some of its best teachers to help parents better understand their children? Some public and parochial schools have caught this spirit and are treating home schools as satellite institutions. Why not have more of this supportive relationship? *The spirit and intent of the law, rather than its letter, should always reign where the needs of children are at stake.* [58, 59, 60, 61]

There need be no fear concerning job losses within our public educational system. Rather, there is urgent need to use more teachers to work with the home, and to give less money and devotion to politically contrived programs that force kids out of their home nests before they are mentally and emotionally ready. And much better informed programs are needed to make more homelike those early schools that are necessary for children whose families cannot or will not care for them. In such schools we need more of the homespun principles and informal methods outlined in this book. We need less of the school readiness programs that are crowding in on our preschools and kindergartens today and stifling the excitement of life and learning in our little children.

We give credit to those many fine parent groups, reputable alternative schools, and church-related organizations who are increasingly offering sound programs for parents who wish to educate their children at home during their early years. Visit and see for yourself how warm and responsive parents provide the greatest early teaching a child can have, by simply being themselves—consistent, alert, and responsive models. Mothers and fathers who read to their children will have children who read. Parents who work with their children will build responsible, dependable, orderly workers.

No schoolroom can match the simplicity and power of the home in providing three-dimensional, firsthand education. The school, not the home, is the substitute, and its highest function is to complement the family. The family is still the social base, and must be, if our society is to survive. Let's leave no stone unturned to guarantee the fullest freedom of the home and the rights of parents to determine the education of their children. It is the "stifling" atmosphere of some public and parochial classrooms, says one New Jersey mother, that turns parents back to the flexibility of the home school.

While some parents prefer home education for reasons of religion, moral influences, and absence of ridicule and rivalry, many like this mother see the home as a "more nourishing place for my child to be, where he can make his own decisions, work out his own problems, and go at his own pace under my personal guidance. Here the social pressures are fewer, yet the neighborhood kids love our home." She adds, "My husband and I intend to maintain control of our family. We saw that we were losing it when our son was in kindergarten. We feared the influence he was bringing home before our other children. We are accountable for our kids, so we decided to retain the authority that goes along with this responsibility."

Well said. The hand that rocks the cradle still rules the world. Let's be sobered at the thought of loosening that grip. And with all respect for the many warm-hearted teachers in many fine schools, let us not forget that the God who designed the kids ordained the family to nest them. And let the school follow after.

CHAPTER TWO

Parents in Charge

The other day an attractive and prosperous young Chicago couple were discreetly brought to visit us by mutual friends who were worried about the young couple's three- and five-year-old daughters, fearing that they were "in trouble." Conventionally enrolled in nursery school and kindergarten, they were already out of control, increasingly irritable and in the words of our mutual friends, "sometimes even obnoxious." The parents told us, "We put them in the best of schools to give them every chance to become academically superior," and because "their socialization is so important to us."

Periodically they felt compelled to apologize to us for the girls' behavior as they ranged all over the house, into everything, with attention spans shorter than a traffic wait at a red light. Yet the parents allowed that our home was "new to them" and they were "just excited."

They felt sorry, they said, for children who could not have the same opportunities as their little girls. With aplomb, they steered the conversation into a stirring discussion of the contrasting horrors of physical child abuse—which was then prominent on the media. Somehow that failed to distract us from the vandalism of their "little treasures" as they raced around our home. They had almost no self-control; they could not sit down and enjoy a book or a toy or a sand box for a few minutes just for the relaxed fun of it.

Our mutual friends had understated the acuteness of the young couple's problem. Yet we were dealing with conventional parents who were responding in conventional ways to conventional themes of rearing very normal children. They were confusing childhood license with freedom, and social pleasure with control. Their license was the kind Webster's calls "freedom without responsibility." And they showed clearly how social pressure enacts charades as both the parent and offspring of conventional wisdom and practice. It insists that since "everyone is doing it," sending little tykes to school somehow is the right thing to do. And its results are in proportion to its presumption. It makes wreckage of most of our children.

We were beginning to get desperate from the little intruders' antics in our cupboards and drawers when we were saved by another five-year-old. She came bounding in from the lake shore, excited about a strangely shaped lichen she had found at the base of one of our trees. She had been living with us for the past two weeks, to relieve her exhausted mother. After introductions around, she quickly settled down in a mature and deliberate manner in the next room as self-appointed hostess to the two little hyperkids.

The contrast in behavior between our five-year-old and the other was so clear that our visitors marveled. "But," my wife Dorothy pointed out, "two weeks ago she was at least as wound up as your girls. She was disorganized and unable to give her attention to anything for more than a moment or two." And then to clinch her point she added, "Her mother is twice-married, twice-divorced, and with psychological problems, and her brothers are living with her own daddy." The little girl had all the seeds of insecurity, but in less than two weeks had responded to warm, consistent care provided continuously by a person who wanted to be her friend.

Wise and Simple Mothering

"But what *did* you actually *do?*" was the eager question. Dorothy replied that she just mothered her—mostly took the child into her homemaking chores, but also played with her, ate with her, read to her, followed a consistent and reasonable pattern at mealtime, saw that she had a good nap and gave her time to run free like a little lamb and also to play alone. In other words, she put her on a track, a constructive program supplying security, warmth, responsiveness, and a sense of purpose and self-worth—a track taking her over her inevitable little ups and downs with surprising smoothness. She felt and quickly became part of our family corporation. Dorothy had given her a very simple model, and that example had already returned its blessings.

Careful indirect questioning brought from the young mother and father the real reasons for their children's hyperactivity, and some conclusions about control. We asked, for example, about their youngsters' readiness to sleep at night, their appetite for nourishing food at mealtime, their elimination and bladder control, their aptness for simple household chores, and their ability to follow through on parental requests. Although sometimes mixed at first, the parents' responses eventually revealed disappointment on all counts: reluctance to go to bed, snacking, churlishness at meal-time, hard stools, bed-wetting, and general indolence and irre-sponsibility. When we got down to points on their behavior in our house, the father quickly and concernedly admitted that it was also "par for the course" in their own home. They had suddenly become aware of their inadvertent pretense.

Socially Pressured Child Abuse

They wondered why they had believed as they did. But it did not take long for this father and mother to recall their own homes and schooling, their own insecurities as children, and the father his sense of rejection when he was sent to kindergarten at four or five (although he "cried to go because all the neighborhood kids were going"). Both recalled the influences of college education classes: "Preschool was the 'in' thing." Then there were articles in magazines, television counsel on child care, trends in federal and state programs, the popular Head Start, the feminist movements and their pressures for mothers to work, and the parental boredom at home which somehow ensues when women are insecure or ill-motivated in their role as homemakers and mothers. Our new friends concluded that they had been effectively brainwashed by a combination of active vested groups, conventional wisdom and their own selfish demands for "freedom."

As we talked on, they came to still other conclusions, starkly different from those of an hour or so before. They decided with us that the greatest horror in child abuse is not usually the deprivation of poverty nor the pummeling brutality on a preschool child nor even the murder of the unborn, however stark that may seem. The most widespread and appalling child abuse is the everyday depressing of the formative mind and sensitive heart by the ignorance, indifference, and ostracism of those who created him. Mental anguish is often less reckoned than physical pain, but for the small child it poses far greater dangers.

The mother and father who *unnecessarily* turn from their youngsters for personal fulfillment or who casually send them away for day care or early institutional life may, without realizing it, be damaging their children. For those who doubt this conclusion, famed World Health Organization's early childhood head, John Bowlby, points out that the child who is occasionally physically bruised by a drunk or confused or frustrated parent still usually has the reasonable certainty that he has family and home and some assurance that he belongs.[7] The former director of the U.S. National Demonstration Center for Early Childhood Education (DCE) in Washington, D.C., Martin Engel, insists that no matter how we rationalize it, "even the best, most humane and personalized day-care environment cannot compensate for the feeling of rejection which the young child unconsciously senses" when he is unnecessarily sent away from home for care by others.[19] It is this mental trauma that Dr. Bowlby and others believe is more damaging in the long run than most physical abuse.

What Really Educates

For the first eight to ten years at least—until their values are formed—most parents, even average parents, are by far the best people for their children. And those that are not, usually can and should be. To be sure, there are areas of child care in which others can outdo parents—such as physicians, nurses, and specialty teachers in music and the arts. But in general the best teacher or care-giver cannot match a parent of even ordinary education and experience. Dr. Marcelle Geber's studies in Uganda proved that even tribal mothers who did not know how to read or write reared children who were more intellectually and socially alert and secure by Western standards than well-educated mothers.[19,25] The difference? Tribal mothers were close to their children. So-called higher class mothers tended to share the care of their children with others.

Dr. Harold Skeels found that even retarded orphan teenagers were excellent "mothers" when they gave consistent affectionate care to orphan babies, and the infants made remarkable gains in mental ability to move on to live normal family lives, while other infants became retarded, or died.[55] Warmth, responsiveness, and consistency are far more important to the young child's learning than is the parent's level of education. Parents must expect more of their children—more helpfulness, more obedience, more self-control—if they want their little ones to be settled and secure.

Most mothers and fathers can provide deeper security, sheerer closeness, sharper instincts, longer continuity, warmer responses, more logical control and more natural examples than the staff of the best care center or kindergarten. Without ever ringing a school bell, monitoring a recess or opening a course-of-study manual or even knowing the inside of a college, their teaching and care in their home are for their children under eight or ten easily superior to the most skilled professors outside it. And a combination of all natural parental advantages will instinctively or with simple and most modest help usually bring out children who excel academically, behaviorally, morally, and socially. This is true even if the children begin school one or more years later at the second, third, fourth, or fifth grade—which is what we firmly believe they should do.

Danger: Caretakers for Hire

This bright and confident young couple were in fact systematically undermining the mental and physical health of their children. By subjecting them to care for hire, at their ages, in school-size groups, they were directly attacking the immature central nervous systems of their little girls. For example, even if you invite over only 10 or 15 little children for a simple party, your four- or five-year-olds will become hyperactive for a day or so and will sleep fitfully for a night or two. But day after day of such group activity and competition for little children, particularly without the instant availability of their mothers or fathers, may take even a greater toll. And this is only the beginning of troubles for the little ones and of trials for their parents in the years ahead.

Children under eight are seldom, if ever, able to reason consistently about why they should or should not behave as parents see best, and sometimes cannot do so until eleven or twelve. So a reasonably consistent, continuing adult example is important if they are to get on a track toward sound character and personality values. This is usually denied them when they leave home for early out-of-home care in the group. Children are nearly always plagued with the inconsistency of adult examples when parents share the modeling with teachers, aides, nannies, and other caregivers.

Especially Little Boys

In Napa, California, Mrs. Isabell Pettit became curious about the real reasons for increased childhood and juvenile delinquency, especially among little boys, so she did a number of studies of Northern California cities and counties. She was aware of the well-established fact, noted earlier, that boys are known to trail girls in maturity a year or so during the early school years and up to three years or so in adolescence. She found among other items that:

1. The earlier that children—boys and girls—go to school the greater the likelihood for dropouts and delinquency.

2. Twice as many boys as girls were suspended during the

elementary years and up to four and a half times as many boys were suspended from high school as were girls.

3. More little boys were admitted early to school than little girls.

Little boys are particularly vulnerable not only because of their comparative immaturity, but also because they tend to receive less warm affection and attention than little girls. Mothers fuss more over their daughters, and tend to want their little boys out from under their feet sooner. The little boy tends to experience more anxiety, more frustration, and more failure just for being, well, a boy. Yet the law is no respecter of sexes. It makes no allowances for maturity in child development. So little boys pay a heavy price for legislative folly, and lady teachers get the blame.

Depending on Peers

At the other end of our country, Cornell University's Urie Bronfenbrenner reported the findings briefly cited in Chapter 1 of an experimental group of 766 sixth-graders, who spent about twice as much of their elective time with their agemates as with their parents.[14] These peer-oriented youngsters did this more from a lack of attention and concern at home than because of pressures or attractiveness of their playmates. When compared with youngsters who spend most of their early years with adults the experimental students were more likely to get into trouble, to rate themselves lower, to have negative views of their peers, to view their parents dimly, and to be pessimistic about their future. Notice that this results more from withdrawal of the parents than of the children. So by our default our youngsters are left to find their habits and values and life styles—the ingredients of their characters—from what Dr. Bronfenbrenner calls the "social contagion" of their peers. And it now is well established that by nature most children are not carriers of sound social values. Peer dependency is a social cancer of our times.[13]

As we refine this manuscript today, a concerned young mother called us from Illinois.

"Dr. Moore," she pleaded, "I need some support."

"How can we help you?" I asked.

"Well, I've been convinced about home schooling ever since I sat in your studio audience on the Donahue Show. My little boy is now five and you can't imagine the pressures I'm getting from neighbors . . ."

"We understand. It happens every day."

"But, I'm sorry to say, I'm also getting the word from my husband. He fears that Jeffrey will feel left out of things if he doesn't go to school. He's afraid Jeffrey will be ridiculed by the neighborhood kids."

"I'm glad he is that concerned about his little son," I replied. "Thank God that you have that kind of husband . . ."

"I am . . . very thankful. That's the reason I'm calling you."

"Please tell him," I answered, "that in virtually every home where parents respond warmly and consistently, and take their children places and make things with them, their home is the social center of the neighborhood. This is the way the Larry Horbinskis found it in Milwaukee (you will remember him also on Donahue). And this is the way it is every day at the Doug and Meg Johnson home in Ridgewood, New Jersey. The neighbor children are quick to see which parents really care. Your problem, if any, will be to have peace from the neighbor kids—they'll like you so well."

"I'm so glad . . ."

"And you will find that when they do go to school, your youngsters will be among the social leaders."

The "IML" (Integrated Maturity Level)

Children's readiness for academic achievement such as reading, writing, arithmetic, and language arts depends a great deal on the maturity of their sensory systems—vision, hearing, taste, touch, smell—on their motor coordination or ability to handle a pencil or chalk and to manipulate small things. It depends also on the development of their brains and central nervous systems, and on their ability to reason consistently from cause to effect—such as to be able to answer *why*; to make judgments of distance, time and space; and to evaluate motives. *

New learnings depend upon related experience. For adults this may come easy, but for the young child without adult experience it takes more time. For most children, reasonable maturity for formal learning seems to bring together or integrate all their senses and organs between the ages of eight and ten or eleven. We call this chronological age period the *Integrated Maturity Level* or IML—the optimum time for most normal children to start school, entering at the level of their agemates at grade three, four, or five. They will quickly catch up and usually pass the children who started earlier. Parents can judge the maturity of their children within the eight-to-ten age range to determine their readiness for school. If there is any doubt, it is usually better to wait.

Your child indeed needs every month or year he can get, up to age eight to ten, to build a rich background of experience on which to base his formal learning. But there is also no substitute for his ability to reason consistently if you want him to know how to think rather than simply to be a repeater of facts; that is, if you want him to learn at a quality level.

Although little girls usually enjoy an advantage, even they do not bring all their learning tools together before age eight. And when little boys are allowed to start at nine or ten in grades three or four or five, they have no trouble keeping up with girls of the same age. Thus little girls and boys both would do well to start at the later ages.

The late dean of America's psychiatrists, James T. Fisher,[21] joins learning psychologists Meredith Robinson,[52] William Rohwer[53] and David Elkind,[17] mentioned earlier, in suggesting that twelve or later would be even better. Dr. Fisher started school successfully at thirteen and vowed that any normal child with a decent home can

---

*Powerful research evidence on early childhood readiness for schooling is provided by the author in the books *School Can Wait* and *Better Late Than Early*, available from The Moore Foundation, Box 1, Camas, WA 98607

do it. Dr. Elkind adds that if there is any correlation between early formal instruction and mental growth it is a negative one.[18]

The value parents place upon their children and the courage they have in facing up to conventional wisdom and social pressures determine how their children will come out in the end. There is no systematic body of research that indicates that young children *who can be provided a good home* will do as well or better if they go to preschool! The child who goes to school later, entering with his age-mates, nearly always comes out better academically, behaviorally, and socially. The emphasis should be on providing a good home. That is what this book is all about.

Academic readiness for schooling is closely related to social readiness. If the child is socially and emotionally ready for school he will be much more comfortable and secure with both the teacher and fellow students. His likely frustrations and embarrassments will be eased and failure avoided. He can handle himself with some independence and ride easily over petty problems which may be mountains—or chasms—for the unready child.

A Special Kind of Socialization

New Jersey researcher John Forester[22] was surprised to find that the social leaders in his high school were usually those who had started school late. Yet such a finding is generally true, if one is thinking of a positive kind of sociability.

A common myth, believed by most of our adult population, indeed suggests the opposite—that children are best socialized by mixing them regularly into groups of children about their own age. Yet if one wants truly positive sociable children who will mature into outgoing, altruistic adults, one will avoid their regular mixing with their peers on a group basis as in preschool or kindergarten or primary school until they are at least eight or ten.

As we have observed earlier, you, the parents, are by far the best socializers of your children. Their behavior outside the home—at church, in the market and with friends—will reflect implicitly the quality of your relationship with them at home. To send them *unnecessarily* to out-of-home care during the first eight years or so before their habits and manners and values are well established will generally dilute and pervert your efforts toward building a positive sociability. This in turn will make your children less secure, more peer dependent, more prone to anxiety, frustration, and learning failure.[11, 15, 20, 24, 43]

Children whose parents are forced by absolute necessity to send their children away for care or to school often seem to understand and to feel less rejected than do those who are unnecessarily sent away. It is as if there were some divine hand over them. But all such children suffer more than those who are allowed to remain in a reasonably secure nest until it is time to fly. It is as if they were little birds fallen or pushed out of the nest before they were ready— frantically, fearfully fluttering around on the ground, unable to make fullest use of their beautiful but unready wings.

At early school they soon find that they must compete for teacher approval, instead of having instant recourse to mother or daddy. They must compete for toys often before they are emotionally able or ready to share. And perhaps worst of all, turned out by their parents, they begin quickly to compete for the attention of their agemates, absorb their language and manners and habits and mores and become dependent on their approval.

When parents try to explain why children should not say certain words or eat certain things, they may not understand, for they are not yet consistently reasonable, or "cognitively ready"—they do not understand fully the "why" of mother's or daddy's explanation. And since "All the kids are doing it," they give the backs of their little hands to their parents' cherished values, and become dependent upon their peers for their value systems. Thus step by step parents lose control, their authority usurped by the school authorities to whom they delegated responsibility for their children. Authority and responsibility usually must be commensurate, so when one is given up the other usually follows. Much learning failure can with expert remedial care be corrected, but with rare exception, when a child loses a sound value system, it is never regained. So peer dependency is a kind of social cancer. Humanly speaking, to try to heal it is like putting a Band-aid on a burned roast.

On the other hand, parents or surrogates who take their children into their daily activities on a warm, continuing consistent basis until they are eight to ten will find that their youngsters generally feel secure as part of the family corporation. Children fed and warmed at the breast are particularly secure. By the time babies are ready to toddle they can be taught to put their toys away in a box in a corner. They begin to identify with the box, to have a sense of neatness, order, and responsibility.

As the years move on they enjoy working with mother and father in the kitchen, in and out of the house, washing the car, gardening. They experience the highest quality of play with warm, responsive parents who also enjoy holding and reading to them, and who allow them time alone to work out their own fantasies and to rest. Such children feel needed, wanted, and depended upon. They sense that they are integral parts in the family corporation. This feeling of belongingness and of the privilege of helping brings a sound sense of self-worth and altruism which are the crucial foundation stones of positive sociability. They move on a single, uncluttered track toward a secure and productive life.

Such children are more deliberate and settled, less inclined to be hyperactive. They often are the babies who will more readily go to you without fear when you are a guest in the home. As young children they are less demanding of their parents, and more likely to feel secure when their mothers and fathers are gone for brief periods. Although more friendly, they are also more independent of peer values as they grow older. In short, they are happier, better adjusted, more thoughtful, competent, and sociable children.

But there is a price to pay. And many psychologists, legislators, policy-makers, and writers think most parents will not pay it. Many of these critics agree that for most families parent education is a greater need than preschool, but insist that our mothers and fathers are so corroded with license (freedom without responsibility) and convention that efforts at reform are exercises in futility. Even the clergy join in this choir of woe. We have moved enough among the ghettoes and the mansions, and the houses in between, to understand this funereal song.

Yet we have found strong courage in many parents among our readers and listeners. When informed of their children's developmental needs and the likely rewards of meeting them, those who are thoughtful and honest and concerned for their youngsters are willing to change their life styles. Many will take a step down in luxury or even economize to the bone in order to guarantee the freedoms—the human rights—of their children to develop naturally as the Creator apparently designed.

Many mothers are giving up their jobs, and fathers are oftentimes modifying their schedules in order to accommodate part or full-time employment for mothers. To those pessimistic child specialists and clergymen who suggest that all is hopeless and the world is so bad and who wait only for the apocalypse, we suggest that one of the elements of the gospel is to help parents to understand and to care for their children. Even the Master said, "Occupy till I come." So we undertake to suggest in the next chapters some well-proven ideas to make happier parents who enjoy their children at home, parents who come to learn that they are the best teachers for their children.

Part Two

STEPS IN PARENTHOOD

CHAPTER THREE

Setting the Stage for Birth

"Getting married and having kids" has long been one of the most enchanting and exciting thoughts for adolescents and young adults. It is easy for us to write these lines now that our two children are grown, and both of them are early childhood specialists. We were fortunate also with our two adopted girls, both happily married nurses. But the facts are that a few simple principles and very earthy (or heavenly) methods can make the difference between delight and despair in the rearing of children.

Yet such dreams have increasingly become nightmares in reality. When young couples see the problems many parents have with their children these days, they are often hesitant to take on the responsibilities of parenthood. Nevertheless, many older couples who have brought up fine children will tell you that their child-rearing days were in fact happy, exciting ones—some of their very best. They will tell you that having children was possibly the most fulfilling experience of their lives. But they had to make up their minds that their children would come first, and they would not make their resolution only a pretense.

While child-rearing is a tremendous and fearful responsibility, it can be the most enjoyable part of your life if you are willing to give it the informed time, energy, and dedication that you would concede to any important project. All phases of the child's life are important, but as with the foundation of a building, the beginnings must be as sound and supportive as we can make them. This basic process begins *before* the child is conceived—with the basic health, disposition, and life style of both parents.

Before the Cells Meet

The first few days and weeks of development of the tiny creature—the fetus—are crucial, so it is dangerous to wait until the ovum embraces the sperm and pregnancy is confirmed before making the necessary preparations. For instance, even the relatively mild German measles suffered by the mother, especially during the first three months of pregnancy can cause deformities in the baby. Although this disease can be prevented by a vaccine, it is not safe for the mother to be inoculated during pregnancy or within two or three months of it. The vaccine may have the same effect on the fetus as the illness itself. Even if the mother was immunized as a child, the protection is not long-lasting. We would advise including it in the premarital doctor's visit or, otherwise, well before pregnancy is anticipated.

Venereal disease, of course, is also well known as a rather serious risk to the fetus. A blood test can easily determine this possibility and treatment should be administered considerably before the probability of pregnancy.

Problems of heredity such as hemophilia (the bleeding disease), RH negative blood, PKU (phenylketonuria) or other diseases known to be among the relatives on either side of the family should also be considered *ahead of time*. You should talk with your physician about the course to be followed and the risks involved.

Eating for the Good (Little) Life

Babies are what they "eat," and they eat what their mothers give them. The diet of the mother before and during pregnancy has a direct influence on the health of her unborn child. For maximum nutrition, simple, varied, natural, high-quality food should be eaten at regular meals. Fresh fruit and vegetables should compose a large part of the diet, with free fats and refined sugar cut to a bare minimum. Animal and vegetable fats in free forms—butter, mayonnaise, cooking oils, and the like—are far less desirable for the new life inside you than foods in their natural forms such as milk, corn, nuts, and beans. Nothing should be taken between meals, at least for healthy mothers, except plenty of water— enough to keep the urine pale—so that the blood will be purified and waste will be eliminated regularly and easily.

There are at least two powerful reasons for this self-control: (1) The stomach is an organ that needs rest between meals. Meals of meat, certain vegetables, nuts, and dairy products take at least five or six hours to digest. Fresh fruits and grains and some vegetables— those grown above ground—usually take about two hours to clear the stomach. (2) Digestive scan studies clearly show that the common habit of taking foods and juices between meals greatly adds to, and often multiplies, the total digestive time in stomach and colon.

The longer food remains in the intestines, the more likely it is to begin to decay rather than to be promptly dispatched by normal digestive processes. This and the likelihood of intestinal impaction or hard bowel movements raise the chances for disease and often contribute to intestinal fistulas or hemorrhoids. Any such problems during pregnancy affect the nutrition and welfare of the unborn child. Malnutrition of the fetus in turn can cause brain damage which may not be reversible, so prospective mothers would do well to learn all they can about good nutrition and eating habits well ahead of time.

Caution should be taken also against an obscure infection that sometimes attacks expectant mothers: toxoplasmosis, which is usually caused by a parasite acquired from eating inadequately cooked meat. Meat must be held at high enough temperatures long enough to kill the infecting organism; in other words, it must be very well cooked. Though the symptoms in the adult may be few and mild, the parasite can enter the body of the unborn child and cause blindness, deformities, and even death.

Important No-No's

There is so much evidence now on the bad effects of smoking, alcohol, and drugs on the unborn baby that caring and aware mothers will turn away from these harmful habits before they plan conception. Pregnancy is not a carefree vacation. There is a particularly critical time between conception and *knowing* that conception has taken place. Just one alcoholic binge at, just before, or just after conception can cause fetal alcohol syndrome, which may bring mental retardation, stunted body size, small head size, and facial abnormalities. Any poisonous or foreign substance in the mother's blood damages to some degree the very beginning of the new life that is being formed inside the mother.

Mothers, Yes, but Fathers Too

But the mother is not the only one responsible for the normal healthy development of the child. It is now also known that the father's sperm can be damaged by his indulgence in alcohol; he thus shares responsibility for avoiding genetic defects or fetal death. Though the sperm is evidently more vulnerable to damage at some stages than at others, the father has no way of knowing when that is, and the greater the amount of alcohol consumed, the greater the potential damage.

With present knowledge it is not too farfetched to assume that unhealthful habits of either the father or the mother can influence the future well-being of their offspring. This is certainly one of the ways, as the Scriptures suggest, that the sins of the fathers are visited upon the children for several generations. No one will ever know how many cases of even slight mental retardation, hearing loss or other problems could have been traced to the diet and life style of the parents at the time of the child's conception. But if you get your life in order well ahead of time you will be the wiser and your child happier for it. A smoking or alcoholic or intemperate father can wreck a child's physical and emotional health.

Nevertheless the influence of the mother's habits on her unborn child is much more powerful and direct than those of the father. She needs to know that every time she takes a puff on a cigarette she is figuratively putting the cigarette to the baby's lips. The same is true of the poisonous effects of alcohol, drugs, or any hazardous drinks such as those containing caffeine or other irritants such as coffee, cola, and some teas. It is even true of any medicine, hormones, or vitamins she takes, substances she breathes and radioactive material she is exposed to. All these are potentially dangerous to the developing baby.

Smoking mothers in fact have significantly more miscarriages, premature births, and congenital malformations than non-smoking mothers. Their babies weigh an average 6 ounces less than the others. Nicotine and other irritants restrict the blood vessels and breathing movements, reducing the oxygen level in the baby's blood. Tobacco also disturbs vitamin metabolism. Though the weight may be quickly regained after birth, the oxygen loss can adversely affect other organs, including the brain. One follow-up study which rechecked such children when they were seven years old found them to be shorter than average in stature, more likely to be retarded in reading ability, and generally rated lower in social adjustment.

Alcohol used by pregnant women is absorbed from the stomach into the bloodstream and through the undeveloped body of the growing fetus. Consistent drinking and smoking by the mother often produces infant alcoholics and drug addicts who must suffer the usual painful withdrawal symptoms as they are weaned away from their addiction.

The Problem Drugstore

In the early 1960s the tragedy of the effects of thalidomide on 5,000 babies born with deformities in Europe alerted the world to the danger of drugs. We are not talking just about illegal drugs. We're talking about the prescription drugs and medicines sold freely over the counter. Thalidomide was a so-called simple sleeping tablet taken innocently by mothers during their pregnancy. Those who are in the process of researching the effects of drugs warn against all such medications, from aspirin and laxatives to antihistamines, antibiotics, or tranquilizers, for they all may have the potential to cause birth defects.

Aspirin is particularly dangerous during the *last* three months of pregnancy because it affects the clotting quality of the blood. Other drugs are especially harmful during the critical first three months of pregnancy. Any drug taken at the time of a certain development in the fetus may alter or damage the normal growth of that body part. For unknown reasons, some harmful substances which find their way into the baby's bloodstream from the mother appear to be at least twice as concentrated as they are in her body. Some also remain longer in the baby's body than in the mother's.

An Emotional Matter

A number of years ago medical science assumed that the emotional state of the mother had no influence on the fetus. The child was considered to be well insulated from the mother's actions and feelings. However, in recent years it has been found that maternal stress, anger, fear, and other unpleasant emotions release certain chemicals and hormones into the blood stream which flows through the placenta, causing irritability to the tiny body within the womb. This may cause the body movements of the fetus to be greatly exaggerated, and the upset often continues much longer than the mother's. This is particularly dangerous in early pregnancy. Fathers can and must make every effort to provide the comfort and security so important to budding mothers.

Many are unaware of the effects of prolonged emotional stress on the fetus. The child may be neurotic before he even sees the light of day. He could have cleft palate or hare lip. He may have pyloric stenosis, a narrowing of the outlet of the stomach sometimes caused by tenseness in the mother. And he is more likely to be a difficult baby to handle, crying more and sleeping less, especially in the neonatal period—the days immediately after birth. Since the brain of the fetus is developing during the first three months, severe stress in the mother at that critical time may even cause mental retardation.

So pregnancy is the time when the husband's tender care of the mother-to-be is especially important. And the mother must redouble her efforts to remain cheerful, contented, and self-controlled. The Master, the Creator Himself, says, "Come unto Me . . . and I will give you rest" (Matt. 11:28). This sense of spiritual security and well-being is the best therapy of all.

Some Healthy Hints

Exercise in the fresh air and sunshine is also crucial in the prenatal program. Spend one or more hours each day out of doors, walking, working, or playing moderately. This not only promotes general good health but may be significant in the ease of the birth process. And constructive work such as gardening seems to have a more therapeutic effect than play. To encourage sound breathing and circulation habits, wear loose clothing, suspended from the shoulders rather than from the waist or hips. And balance out your clothing, covering your legs and arms as thoroughly as the rest of the body in cool weather. This may sound old-fashioned, but it accomplishes several marvels: it assures proper circulation of the blood to the placenta which protects and nourishes the growing baby, and it cuts colds and other infections. Chilling of the extremities causes constriction of the blood vessels and reduced general circulation, which opens the gate for all manner of infection. Warm limbs, for example, are vital to a healthy chest.

The importance of rest and sleep should not be underestimated, as well as the regularity of the daily schedule. Eight hours of sleep at night in a well-ventilated room with at least an hour's rest during the day will help you maintain the serene emotional state of mind that tends to produce a more sweet-tempered child. Adequate exercise will give more meaning to your sleep, and this efficiency will help you avoid the chronic tired feeling that demands more sleep than should be necessary.

Since we are orienting this book to the education of both parent and child, we must tell you now that when you follow this prenatal counsel you lay a strong foundation in your child for the greatest possible intelligence and learning ability and all-round adjustment. Babies in the womb are spectators at quite a concert. They are said to be able to hear at about their fourth month of development, listening to a symphony of other body sounds punctuated by the bass of the mother's heartbeat. But don't rely on reading literary masterpieces or math or science textbooks out loud to make your baby brighter. And to play tapes with recorded facts and classical music will have a desirable effect on the child only as it stimulates your own optimism or quiets your spirit. Because your child is a total person—an integrated whole—you can be sure that anything which affects his body or nervous system affects all parts of him— mentally, emotionally, socially, and morally.

When the Baby Exits

Hospital routine and the events connected with the birth process itself have been getting a great deal of attention in recent years. We now know that the health and disposition of the infant is influenced by the circumstances surrounding its delivery. The baby whose father and mother have planned carefully for his coming-out party will almost always be a healthier, happier child. The work of such physicians as Robert Bradley,[9] Barry Brazelton,[10] Marshall Klaus,[33] Fernand Lamaze,[34] and Frederick Leboyer[36] provide convincing and delightful evidence. Don't underestimate this precious experience, whether you are the mother who gave birth or the father who gave her tenderest care.

Dr. Leboyer, a French physician, has become well-known for his objection to noise, bright lights, and separation of mother and child immediately after birth. A follow-up study of 1,000 babies delivered by his careful, natural methods show that they are more contented, alert, and free from feeding problems and from rashes and other skin problems than babies delivered by traditional methods. Marshall Klaus strongly stresses immediate closeness. Doctors Bradley and Brazelton also strongly warn against even the least of drugs and their danger to the tiny one down inside mother, a danger that lingers at least until the cord is cut. The child of the drug-free birth is almost always the most lusty and responsive, the most enthusiastic little sucker for mother's nipples from the start.

Studies have proven that putting the baby immediately to nurse at the mother's breast usually has long-term advantages for both. It is well known that animal babies nurse almost immediately and that animal mothers who are temporarily deprived of their off-spring often demonstrate rejecting behavior or do not allow them to return to the breast at all. Though the higher intelligence of human mothers should not allow such obvious rejection, prompt interaction of mother and child at this crucial point lays the groundwork for bonding of mother and child, permanently influencing the behavior of both. Further, a Brigham Young University professor, Dr. Camilla S. Wood, suspects that infants withheld from feeding for twelve to sixteen hours by traditional hospital routines may suffer from hypoglycemia and possible brain damage.[64]

The combined hormonal action of birth and breast feeding make both mother and baby highly receptive to each other. There should be plenty of time for getting acquainted with each other through seeing, hearing, touching, smelling, and tasting. Though the mother is essentially responsible for initiating interaction with her child, she is also affected by the infant's response. This early intimacy helps establish a good breast-feeding relationship, and it has been found that such a baby rarely has colic or feeding problems.

The immediate breast-feeding method solves some obstetrical problems for the doctor and mother as well. It tends to prevent hemorrhaging from the womb, helps in the ejection of the placenta, and facilitates the return of the uterus to normal size.

Most young couples who together have experienced a natural type of childbirth with rooming-in during the hospital stay are excited about the positive effects it has brought them. The mother who is totally awake and knows for sure that she has borne her child from her own body seems to acquire a special, lasting thrill of ownership and commitment that many anaesthetized mothers do not seem to feel. It has long been felt that mothers who must have Caesarean delivery are deprived of a certain closeness to their offspring. The participation of the fathers also involves them more intimately and sooner than otherwise and tends to create in them not only more empathy with their wives but also a continuing deeper and more tender love and interest in their offspring. As an incidental but significant side effect, natural childbirth seems to strengthen the marriage, especially in both the wife's attitude toward her husband and his toward her. She views him as stronger, more competent, and masculine than does the average wife who experiences conventional childbirth. He has a closer sense of birth than is otherwise possible.

Again, one of the greatest advantages of natural methods is the absence of drugs. Whatever drug is given to the mother to aid in her delivery is passed on to the infant through the placenta. The mother's full-functioning liver can detoxify the drug rather quickly. But the baby's liver is already loaded up with the task of breaking down extra blood cells to eliminate the jaundice new babies normally realize right after birth. And his kidneys are not ready to handle drugs as an adult's can. So he is often too doped up and weak to nurse well at the breast, and often fails to stimulate an adequate flow of milk. This lack of responsiveness robs both mother and child of important experiences in those first few days together, for early mother-child bonding is essential to the child's healthy mental attitudes and influences his ability to form good interpersonal relationships later in life. The damage to these affectional ties is even more serious than the feeding problem. There is also evidence that such drug use causes babies to have more sleep problems, that is, they sleep for shorter periods, cry more, and are more wakeful at night.

The closer to nature's plan in regularity, simplicity, and warm affection the child is born, the brighter are your prospects for a happy child and the more likely his prospects for a fulfilling life. We plan carefully when we mate a thoroughbred filly or heifer. We are cautious about the documentation and care of our pedigreed dog. Nor would we if possible consider any but nature's own ways in caring for fish or plants or birds. Yet none of these has the reasoning capacity of the child to relate to his parents, his environment, and his God. Our plans for his development and survival should be as high and as sacred as the purpose of the Creator who designed him.

CHAPTER FOUR

Getting a Good Start: The Newborn

The computer technicians must be sure that all the rules are followed or the results will be "garbage." So with humans: babies are made by mama computers, with daddies in on the programming. Yet the complexity of the young child's body and brain make a computer look like a twenty-five cent toy. If the manufacturer specifies a certain quality of oil or tape or electricity or supplies, we expect to comply or sacrifice efficiency and his guarantee of sound operation. So it is with a fine car or camera or watch. So, and infinitely more so with the child, we must give the most earnest attention to the Creator's natural prescriptions if we hope to turn out a creature to match our dreams. And this is teaching that the parent can do best.

Homemade Nipples

The breast is a crucial factor in teaching the child a vital self control. About one infant in four in the United States is presently breast fed on a regular basis, and the proportion is increasing. The baby who is fortunate enough to be nursed at the breast not only enjoys the positive psychological benefits of special skin-closeness with his mother but also gains added protection from disease through the antibodies and enzymes contained in mother's milk. His natural diet includes the "bifidus factor," a body product which encourages the growth of "good bacteria" in the intestines, but which is absent in the usual bottle formula involving cow's milk or other milks.

Milk from mother's breast forms a fine, flaky curd in the stomach, while cow's milk typically may form curds the size of the end of your finger. Mother's milk digests faster and more easily. It also helps to prevent allergic reactions and skin disorders, and there is less likelihood of obesity in later life.

An advertisement for a particular brand of milk once stated that it came from "contented" cows, suggesting an important reason for its high quality. The truth is that the disposition of the mother as well as her diet and life style do affect the quality of her milk. If she is nervous and high-strung, under stress or emotionally upset in any way, the amount and digestability of her milk will be influenced adversely.

Recently Dorothy volunteered to care for a ten-month-old child while her mother, Marsha Anderson, whom she'd just met, left for about ten or fifteen minutes. Actually Mrs. Anderson had intended to leave the baby in the room alone. Though the baby girl was in a strange crib, with a strange woman in a strange room, she smiled, cooed, and played as happily as could be. When the mother returned, Dorothy spoke to her.

"She seems so well-adjusted and secure!"

"It's because she's breast-fed," the mother replied. "My first one wasn't and there is a real difference. I'd heard this from other mothers," she added, "but didn't know it made such a difference until I tried it."

Unfortunately the picture is not always so well defined. Breast-feeding alone does not guarantee a serene child. It is the whole bonding process of mother and baby that instills this serenity and trust. Yet the intimacy of breast-feeding is one powerful way to help establish the bond. And its omission often poses problems. In this case the baby was happily willing to let her mother go because she was confident that she would soon be back. This strong and basic step toward positive socialization and personality development is one whose value many parents do not recognize. This baby's close attachment to her mother prepared her to relate well to others. On the other hand, babies deprived of adequate mother love are usually forced into making and breaking attachments with a variety of others until some refuse to make any attachments at all, for fear of being hurt again. They eventually become incapable of trusting anyone fully; they are insecure and often damaged for life—emotionally, socially, and often intellectually.

The mother also reaps some personal benefits from breast-feeding, apart from having a better-adjusted child. Convenience is probably her most practical advantage. During the trying time after birth, no scrubbing, sterilizing, preparing, or shopping is required for baby's meals—no need even to heat a bottle in the dark hours when you're disoriented and bleary-eyed. The loving, close, one-to-one relationship of mother and child ties the heart strings a little tighter for both of them and gives the mother a special feeling of the uniqueness and dignity of womanhood designed for her by a loving God. In addition, breast-feeding helps her body to return faster to normal condition, decreases the possibility of hemorrhaging in the uterus, and apparently even lessens the chances of developing breast cancer in later years.

Mother—and Father—at the Controls

Because some children have suffered from lack of love, harsh discipline, and even injury, there is a very strong push these days to establish early bonding of mother and child and that love and trust which are so very basic to a child's emotional security. This is vital. The infant cannot survive without love. It is as vital to happy childhood as breath, food, warmth, sleep, and daily work and play. Natural childbirth, rooming-in, and breast-feeding are excellent ways to enhance this early, close mother-child-and-father tie. But some of the permissiveness and indulgence that goes with this idea is questionable.

The promoters of this theory insist that there is absolutely no way to spoil an infant with love. We agree; the little one must have continuous loving in order to develop that basic security which is fundamental to his emotional health. But while *true love is selfless, it is not indulgent!* Baby is not mature enough to set his bounds. Even mother birds and animals know this, and they maintain control. Love sees the child's ultimate best good and is not in opposition to discipline. Love builds discipline based on self-control. Love without discipline is not love at all. Before you dismiss this idea as old-fashioned, please read carefully on.

For the newborn, we do not use the word *discipline* as we normally do for older children and adults. We do not scold or punish for failure to obey. Rather in the years before reason is fully developed, it is training of the most fundamental kind—much as the mother animal *trains* her young. It is so subtle that it might be called "unconscious" education. *This is largely accomplished by the regularity of the baby's schedule* along with wise, consistent but gentle firmness with all infant demands. Immediately after birth there may be some flexibility, with gradual changes in the schedule. But as soon as possible a common-sense routine which fits the family as well as the infant should be developed, with the mother's experience and wisdom in control, not the baby's whims. The baby's bath, naps, meals, playtime, and bedtime should be pretty much the same day after day. These regular events are his rules in action. And he understands them more than most parents know. In a sense this requires more self-discipline for the parent than for the child.

Changes are made gradually and deliberately by the mother as the baby grows. The baby is not allowed to be a dictatorial little Napoleon. Of course, he does not see that he is so demanding. He does not realize that he is depriving you of your rights by his selfishness or that he is hurting himself. So you must provide the wisdom and the control. Such regularity and consistency provide the child great security as well as the beginnings of self-control. They give him a sound developmental track which is as important to a child as to the efficiency of a fast train. Lack of such routine always carries the risk of a permissiveness that is difficult to reverse without emotional pain. Since the formation of character begins by day one, it is cruel to let wrong habits be developed, and hope to change them later.

Too many parents do not enjoy their children because of their wrong handling from the very first. When the little ones become too demanding, sometimes to the point of being tyrranical, parents just can't cope with them. Some otherwise loving parents then even physically abuse the child.

The need to establish right habits early in no way implies harshness, neglect, or lack of an intimate, loving relationship. Babies should not be allowed to be angry and miserable. On the contrary, such management demands great tenderness, consistency, and love. It should in no way damage or destroy the close mother-child bonding or the child's emotional health.

We don't know any babies who have complaints about the regularity of their bathtime, but their naturally self-centered, untrained desires can run mother a merry chase when it comes to feeding times unless she is in control. The currently popular "demand feeding" developed when the pendulum swung to the opposite extreme from the old rigid by-the-clock routine which also often eliminated breast-feeding, fondling, and cuddling. What we are concerned with are too many or too frequent feedings which are not really needed, but are used to substitute for other needs, possibly even stomach distress which often is better treated with a drink of water and a temporary rest from food. Don't feed your child every time he cries—regardless of intervals. Often what he needs is some other type of attention. Let's be careful about confusing food with wisdom, consistency, and love.

In order to regulate the baby's feeding schedule he may need much holding, entertaining, soothing, and diverting. But with most normal babies, their requirements are not overwhelming. They usually adapt very quickly to regularity—a schedule which fits their rhythm as well as the family routine. There is no reason for the baby to decide to have his meal at an inconvenient time for the rest of the family. He doesn't necessarily have to be awakened to stay in his routine, but if it is appropriate for the mother's sake, you can be sure he will not object.

Although our personal methods do not constitute a scientific sampling, a special experience Dorothy had may serve as an illustration of how easily a newborn can adjust to reasonable circumstances. At the time Dennis, our first baby, was born in an army hospital in California, I was an army officer in the South Pacific. When Dennis was five days old, the officer in charge of the maternity ward, a brilliant Jewish pediatrician from New York, visited Dorothy. She and the baby were to leave that day.

"Mrs. Moore," he said, "for the good of both your child and you, see that each night you get a good unbroken sleep."

"You mean I shouldn't get up with my baby?" she asked, more than a little surprised.

"That's exactly what I mean. You have a healthy, normal child . . ."

"But what about his feedings?"

"You haven't been feeding him here in the middle of the night, have you?"

"No, I guess I haven't. I never thought of . . ."

"Unless he has some special problem," the physician instructed, "like colic or some other reason for unrest, let him go back to sleep."

"You mean if he cries? Suppose he's hungry?"

"If you feel you have to give him something, give him a little water. Diaper him if necessary. Change his position or pat him to let him know you are there. Pretty soon he'll figure it's not worth waking up."

Dorothy thanked him gratefully.

"You will be a better mother," he said, in departing, "and a lot happier with your little boy. By starting now you won't have to undo something you've established. And don't worry that he won't grow!"

We didn't. And he grew. To six feet two and one hundred and ninety pounds.

It is better to keep things moving systematically in the daytime than to have baby awake and hungry at night. He can be gently maneuvered into schedules which allow for others' freedom as well as his own, and except in cases of special physical handicaps, this can start at day one. Within two or three weeks of birth, most healthy infants can learn to sleep the night through. If they awaken, offer them a little warm water. In most cases they will soon find it is not worth the bother to awake. And rested parents will find them much less of a strain. Only recently our daughter somewhat dubiously accepted our counsel with her firstborn. She has been a more rested mother since.

We don't want to change that kind of parenthood which includes tender, loving physical care, and helps to establish child security and trust. We just want to prevent problems by combining these loving qualities with equally loving methods that enhance the youngster's health, intellect, and personality. This gives a happy balance—the best of both worlds. Parenting need not be the chore that so many parents make it, with endless intrusions into their schedules by innocent but uncontrolled babes. Regularity and rest for the baby mean enjoyment and rest for his parents.

The Digestion Go-Round

Besides the need for regularity as a basis for early indirect discipline, health is vitally affected. Irregularity saps baby's brain forces, disturbs his disposition, and damages his all-round development. As we have implied in the preceding chapter, the interval between feedings should be long enough to allow the stomach fully to digest the former feeding and have a little rest before the next feeding. Otherwise, the stomach may be required to do more than it can handle without distress. Fermentation, indigestion, and stomach upsets often result. Since mother's milk digests faster than cow's milk, the intervals between feedings for the breast-fed baby should be relatively shorter. In either case it takes *about* 3 or 4 hours for the normal, healthy baby to need another feeding. But whatever interval is determined to be appropriate should be *regular and should be lengthened as the baby grows older.*

The Mercy of Scheduling

Sometimes when feeding time should be delayed in order to give the baby's tummy a little longer to rest, a drink of water, a change of position, a dry diaper, or other diversions will do the trick.

Babies forget quickly what it was they wanted and any reasonable attention provides a satisfactory substitute. Even carrying the baby around some during the day is better than having to pace the floor with him at night because his digestion is upset from irregular feedings. Often when he cries it is not food that he needs. If you feed him just to keep him quiet, you will also be teaching him a negative idea—that food is the cure for all of life's ills. *Delaying the gratification of wants or needs is one of the first and most important steps in self-control, the key to a sense of self-worth and positive sociability.*

The Biological Time Clock

Systematic physical care is consistent with the research on "circadian" or body rhythms. In a conversation a few years ago with Dr. Gunther Hildebrandt, world authority in this field at the University of Marburg, we learned the importance of body rhythms as essential to the well-being of the individual from the earliest years. In a sense, the human body is under law in the same way as are the heavenly bodies that control the cycles of night and day, the months and years. Perhaps the most commonly known and dramatic example is jet lag. Crossing several time zones in one day can cause otherwise inexplicable fatigue and difficulty with logical reasoning. One of our traveling friends who ignored these principles ended up in the hospital with all the symptoms of a heart attack. He actually had no serious heart problem at all; his body was simply reacting to the drastic changes in his eating and sleeping times.

Study of circadian rhythms indicates that they begin before the child is born. After birth the feeding rhythm is the first to be established and calls for reasonable regularity, changing gradually in intervals as the infant grows older. The baby is well prepared to adapt to a feeding schedule. In fact, if born in a hospital, he usually has already adjusted to a feeding routine before being brought home. Parents who then choose to feed on demand every time the baby is restless or cries should expect a disorganized situation of their own making.

The quality of the relationship between the baby and his parents or other care-givers is the most essential ingredient in establishing sound early organization of the biological time clock. Obviously then, parents need to provide loving, tender, warm, and responsive care from the moment of birth, without forgetting the firmness and consistency which bring a happy balance.

Tuck-in Time

We should not underestimate the newborn's sensitivity, alertness, and readiness to adapt to his environment. Regular naptime and bedtime are also essential to his basic training and health. A normal, healthy, well-nourished new baby can be taught that when he is put into his bed, it is time for him to go to sleep. He should have plenty of loving, touching, cuddling, and warm, consistent responses to his needs all day long. He should have been bubbled, freshly diapered, and fed before bedtime. He should not be too warm nor too cold, and you should be sure he has no pains or tummyache—from being fed every time he cried all day or for any other reason. But if *all* of these basic needs have been met, what other need does the baby have except sleep? He likes being loved, carried, and attended to, and may protest when he is put down. He certainly does not know yet when enough is enough. And it is up to you to teach him. On the basis of educated common-sense, awareness of what his real needs are and of his future good, you have to decide what is best. By your quiet, firm tone of voice and your *consistent,* loving manner you should convey your decision. Then he should be left to go to sleep.

If your baby is bottle-fed, cuddle him in your arms even after he is old enough to hold his own bottle. Bubble him and then put him in his bed if it is bedtime or naptime. We always placed our babies on their tummies so they could burp themselves naturally. There is some evidence that babies sleep better, don't cry as much, and are not as restless when they are put down on their tummies rather than their backs.[8] Never put a baby to bed with his bottle if you want him to have good sleep habits. If from the very first going to bed is a matter of course and never open to question, you will save yourself many problems. Don't worry about letting the baby cry once his needs are met. If he is a healthy child he will learn who is in charge.

Bottled Risks for Crybabies

Another disadvantage to lulling the infant to sleep with a bottle is the problem of early tooth decay which dentists call "bottle-cavity syndrome." This is commonly found among babies who go to sleep with a bottle of milk or juice. As soon as the baby falls asleep, the natural saliva flow diminishes and the undigested juice is left around the teeth, eventually causing decay. Young children who are allowed to carry a bottle around with them to suck on and off for a long period of time run the same risk.

A mother can generally identify the meaning of her baby's cries. These become more varied in tone and intensity soon after birth. The baby should have the opportunity, of course, to exercise his lungs occasionally, and parents should take a certain amount of this in stride as long as real needs are being met. The cry of pain or real distress should be answered immediately. Even then, the answer may not be to pick the baby up if it is in the middle of the night. Check him for an open pin, feverishness, or other obvious discomfort first and try to soothe him by gently patting his back and talking lovingly to him. If he is actually ill or cannot be comforted in a reasonable time, try giving him a drink of water and do whatever is necessary to help him. Keep your night effort as brief as possible. Except in critical circumstances, don't rock him, walk him, take him in bed with you, or feed him unless you elect to have a needlessly broken nightly routine for some time to come.

As much as possible, your baby's actual needs should be anticipated so that he doesn't need to cry for the attention he deserves. This lessens his motivation for crying and reinforces pleasantness. He may even resort to less objectionable baby noises to communicate his needs. In general, the more love and attention you give when your baby is happy and pleasant, the more you will reinforce these good qualities. On the other hand, the more you respond to his crying, the more you will teach him that crying gets him what he wants when he wants it, and both you and he will be the ever-lasting victims of his demands.

The Little Psychologist

We know of a few mothers who carry their very young babies around some of the time during their waking hours in a heavy cloth support that holds the infant close to their breasts or their backs and keeps their arms free for other activities. This is one way to keep baby happy and close as long as it does not interfere with his regular sleeping times in his own bed or with his necessary exercise. Too much holding or carrying can interfere with his physical development. Plastic infant-seats are convenient for keeping the baby safe nearby for short periods while he is awake, but for actual carrying, body-closeness is by far the preferable technique.

Notice that we used the qualification "normal" in the training for good sleep habits. Babies born to smoking, drinking, or drug-taking mothers might not be normal in the best sense of the word. Even a poor maternal diet or emotional stress during pregnancy can damage the child's nervous system. We also know that difficult labor and respiratory depression from medication used for the mother during the birth process often cause babies to have sleep problems. They tend to sleep for shorter periods and to be more fussy and wakeful. Some babies are definitely more difficult than others with no apparent reason. Others who may not have the advantage of breast-feeding could be among the 15 percent or more who are allergic to cow's milk. This could cause unusual problems temporarily until a digestible formula is found. Soybean or similar vegetable milks are often life-saving answers for this.[42] Some adaptation would surely need to be made for these special cases, but we believe that in general the principles of discreet, tender, consistent control still apply. It has been found that holding the baby securely but not jiggling him, and stroking him *gently* will soothe and calm him. But, again, don't feed him unless he is actually *needing* food.

The baby is highly sensitive to the mother's emotional state. If she is relaxed and confident, he will usually respond in kind. But if she is overly anxious and tense, he will likely have problems. He may cry unduly and have trouble eating or sleeping. He will even react to the way he is held. If he is handled gently but firmly with good support of his neck and head, he will feel secure. The snug wrapping of the receiving blanket has the same purpose at first. He has not been used to having his arms and legs free in the womb and he needs to become accustomed gradually to this freedom. Yet he should not be hung carelessly by his arms, for his little shoulders may easily be dislocated. Husky fathers should especially take note!

The Challenge of Consistency

The power of the parents' behavior is actually quite awesome, for they have the capacity to mold the habits and personality of the child in very specific ways. Their basic example comes across most strongly, but their treatment of the infant can to a large degree determine his sleep habits, eating habits, emotional stability, and personality development.

We know that eventually most babies naturally sleep through the night, but we have counseled with many mothers who have been worn to a frazzle by the continuing 24-hour demands of their babies. Many mothers are still being awakened two or three times each night by children who are six to sixteen months old. Often they are well-nourished, healthy children and don't need any extra feedings. They usually take only a slight amount of milk, for they are not really hungry. They are simply habituated to expecting this indulgence.

When our Kathleen was born, we handled her as Dorothy had been told to deal with Dennis. We have since found out that many pediatricians recommend this, for it is considerate of both mother and child. We discovered by firsthand experience what we later found to be an important law of the mind: if you are firm and consistent enough in denying something so as to remove all hope that you will relent, your baby will soon cease to desire it and he will turn his attention to something else. The small baby is highly sensitive to the way he is handled and learns quickly whether or not his parents are decisive in the face of persistent crying. He will control you if he can. It is small wonder that so many mothers tire early of their children's care.

The development of these good sleeping habits without a hassle paid good dividends for us. Although we do not necessarily recommend extended traveling with babies or small children, circumstances required us to do a lot of it when our children were little. We traveled across the United States by train and auto, then round trip to Hawaii by ship, and later to Japan by ship—all by the time our daughter was three years old. We learned to do with some inconveniences for the sake of family togetherness. On her first trip, when she was three months old, Kathleen's bed was a dresser drawer in a Detroit hotel. We could put her and Dennis down for a nap or bedtime in a strange bed, on the floor, or on the seat of an airplane or train, and in short order they would go to sleep. It was a test both of their security and obedience. The exercise began when they were born.

Little Suckers and Other Expedients

You must make up your mind if you want a thumb sucker and the dental bills that frequently result from this undesirable habit, which can be early prevented much more simply than it can be later cured. If the baby is getting the loving care we have described, and in sufficient quantities, he should have no real need for sucking his thumb. A temporary lapse because of hunger, fatigue, or boredom should be quickly nipped in the bud before the habit becomes established. It may look cute to some naive parents but it does little good and can be a costly crutch. It typically starts at bedtime, so a sleeping bag or other means of restraining the baby's hand from reaching his mouth can easily be used. As we have mentioned, baby's memory is short and any frustration he may feel will soon disappear. We know by experience that it works, if begun at the very first signs of the habit. Many parents have thanked us for this suggestion.

Nor is a pacifier really necessary either, especially for the breast-fed baby. There is a danger that both child and parent can become overly dependent on it. And, as with thumbsucking, dentists often protest that the pacifier can alter the normal structure of the mouth and teeth. It makes a great deal of unnecessary business for orthodontists and can sometimes cost as much as damage by thumb. It may also encourage an artificial desire for oral gratification, as seen in those who seem always to be sucking on mints, or tobacco, smoking cigarettes or chomping on a cigar. However, if the baby is not breast-fed and really needs more sucking or has colic, a pacifier might sometimes be justified as a temporary solution. It can usually be dispensed with more easily than thumbsucking.

In general it is best not to start anything you do not wish to continue—rocking, yes, for loving and soothing, but not for getting baby to sleep for regular naps or bedtime. As the baby grows past the first few weeks and months be careful about bringing him into bed with you while you nurse him. This establishes a habit which the child may find difficult to break. He will easily come to demand your bed instead of his. And there is also the real possibility that you—as many parents have done—may fall asleep and roll over on him.

Take special care with baby's bath. Some infants seem to love their baths from the very first, but some experience a strong natural fear of falling if they feel insecurely held, and some fear the noise of running water. Some mothers use thin cotton gloves to be able to hold baby's slippery body more firmly. Get all the equipment ready and run the water ahead of time until your baby becomes accustomed to the bath routine. Use a rubber mat if the bottom of the small tub or basin is slippery. Hold him securely and immerse him gradually and gently so that he can get the feel of the water.

Talk calmly and assuringly as you proceed. If the baby shows strong resistance to the usual method of bathing, try sponge bathing him on a towel spread over a table or a drainboard for a few days or weeks. Some doctors feel that until the baby is creeping and picking up dirt from the floor, three regular baths a week with local washings as needed, such as at diaper changes and feedings, are more likely to keep the infant's skin from getting dry and irritated. The number of baths also depend on the weather and other conditions. Loss of body heat is often a problem during cold weather, but more than one bath might make baby more comfortable when the weather is very warm. For the sake of mother's back, all this normally should be done at counter height.

The most fundamental learnings of the newborn child are the sense of belonging and security established by the continuity of loving care, the early organization of body rhythms into a routine that forms the basis for sound health and the beginnings of self-control, along with early prevention of bad habits and the establishment of good ones. Simplicity, consistency and firm, tender care must take precedence over indulgence and expediency, no matter how common and self-assured your neighbor's practices seem to be.

CHAPTER FIVE

That Crucial First Year

Babies are sparkling sponges with eyes, ears, fingers, noses, and tongues. They soak up sights, sounds, textures, smells, and tastes. Everything that the baby sees, hears, or experiences teaches him something. And his physical development is dramatic. Yet it is not safe or wise to try to hurry him in his accomplishments or to over-stimulate him. Pressure may actually delay his normal development or make him tense or nervous. Wise, imaginative, patient, and in-tuitive parents are aware of baby's efforts and growing stages and will give him practice to expand and improve his abilities as they appear. They respond lovingly always, firmly where necessary, and with some imagination. This is teaching of the highest order. The warm, responsive, consistent parent is the world's best teacher.

Hearing

Within a very short time listening is one of the things the newborn can do best. His favorite sound is usually mother's voice. He will enjoy your lullaby or soft singing even if you aren't a great singer. Sing often and adapt your tunes to the activity at hand. Make up your songs as you go. He won't worry if you are sharp or flat, nor will he criticize your tune. He'll love it. Songs or happy talk will help to distract him if changing or dressing are frustrating to him. Musical sounds such as wind chimes or a music box and soft recordings of good music are helpful some of the time, too, if there is plenty of peace and quiet to balance. The newborn needs comforting and soothing rather than excitement or entertainment, so he won't appreciate rock music, bright or flashing lights, loud noises, or jiggling. Jiggling—a common parental device—may even accentuate his natural fear of falling or cause him to lose part of his dinner. Cuddling, patting, and soft talking or singing in a relatively quiet atmosphere are best for his tender nerves.

Too many or too loud sounds—television, records, machines, etc.—can overstimulate him and damage his hearing as well. He may react negatively to block out what is irritating to him. Unfortunately, he is not yet able to be selective. He not only turns off the noise but also certain sounds that are valuable to his learning. These might be speech sounds that he needs for language development or the voices of insects, birds, wind, or rain that orient him to nature and the out-of-doors. They may be ordinary household sounds such as a clock ticking, a door opening or closing, water running, or preparations for a meal. As he learns to identify these sounds with particular events, he fills in his knowledge about his everyday world, adjusting to it and forming his background for learning. He also associates voices about him with sights, smells, tastes, and textures that enliven his world. Notice how quickly he hears and identifies even such apparently insignificant sounds as mother's footsteps, and responds to her approach.

Beginning to See

The new baby's eyes should be shielded from sunlight and bright lights. At first he can use only one eye at a time but will learn to focus both eyes together by the end of the first month. Then he will enjoy looking at bright-colored or shiny objects hung on one or both sides of his crib which can attract his attention when he wakes up. Homemade ones will do. Suspend a picture of a smiling face mounted on cardboard, or hang colored plastic cups, small aluminum foil pans, or other household items. Include a bell which he can hit to make it tinkle. This will tempt him to play, kick, and coo rather than cry when he awakes. Be sure there are no small parts to come loose that your baby might put into his mouth and choke on, or any sharp edges to cut him.

A few weeks after birth, your baby's skill in swallowing will be smoother than at first and while nursing he will stop his sucking for a few seconds at somewhat regular intervals. He will do some looking during these pauses, particularly if there are objects close by to look at. These delays indicate the very beginnings of self-control and an increased interest in his environment.

He also likes to watch large moving forms. His favorite ones are usually people, including his own reflection in the mirror, although he does not recognize it as his own image until he is around six months old. At about three months he becomes interested in hands and feet—others' as well as his own. Later you will help him discover that most external parts of his body come in pairs. He will point them out and compare them with yours even before he can talk. A daily tour around the house or yard to see, hear, and touch whatever is safe and available can start early, too. This is a good delaying tactic for meals, therapy for restlessness or boredom, and a learning activity as well.

When it is good weather, your baby can be in a protected place such as a porch where he can see the sky or shadows and fluttering leaves. When he can sit up, he will like to watch whatever animals are around—a caged bird or a fish in a bowl—a cat or puppy to feel. Care should be taken, however, about cleanliness, for baby's hands can carry germs quickly to his mouth. Unfortunately cats and dogs carry germs and parasites which could be damaging to baby's health.

Around the age of seven or eight months your baby will like to play "where" games. If you ask "Where is Johnny (brother)?", "Where is daddy?", "Where is birdie?", he will respond by looking. If you point, he will learn to point, too. For very short periods of time this game can be transferred to a book with simple pictures. Often a homemade book of simple, familiar, and realistic items is better than a store-bought one. You can make pages of cloth or heavy cardboard and sew or tie them together. After you ask a question like "Where is the kitty?", answer it by pointing or using baby's finger to point, saying "There is the kitty" with expressive inflection. As you repeat this game daily he will soon mimic your tone of voice and point by himself. If you know a simple song or rhyming verse or can make one up, you may be able to lengthen his attention span for this activity.

And you can start reading to him any time now. For many years to come, book reading while you hold him closely on your lap will be a very special time of learning for him, both intellectually and emotionally. This should be a daily activity, eventually taking up twenty or thirty minutes. Teach your child to handle books tenderly, almost reverently. He must not confuse them with playthings. They are not to be piled into a toy box or thrown around. It is easy for children to be destructive and wasteful unless you teach them how to care properly for all their belongings. (See Appendix 2 for reading list.)

Soon your baby will be especially interested in things that move and he can follow with his eyes—a ball rolling toward him, moving animals, birds, people, or cars. Small objects will attract his attention and he may study them intently—buttons on a dress or shirt, bits of string or lint. Throwing, banging, and manipulating various safe household objects promotes mental and motor (muscle coordination) growth as he inspects their size, shape, colors and action when they fall or roll, or fail to roll. While we do not condemn the buying of playthings, we have observed that commercial toys are generally unnecessary for children to whom ordinary things are exciting and new: spoons, pans, unbreakable dishes and cups, spools, and plastic containers. Take care that loose, small objects do not get into your child's mouth. We almost lost our little girl when she found a stray marble under a neighbor's chair and put it in her mouth. It lodged in her throat and only a miraculous cough pushed it out after we had tried and failed with other first-aid methods.

Talking and Getting Along

Your baby is definitely a social creature who likes to be talked to. Though his early smiles are only reflexes, he will surprise you with a real smile as early as three or four weeks if you smile at him first. He will continue to smile more and cry less if his smiles get more attention than his cries. He has plenty of other sounds he experiments with to communicate his needs and you who are close to him will learn what he means. Smacking his lips or sticking out his tongue may indicate hunger. Squirming or throaty vocal sounds may signal restlessness. If you respond patiently and wisely to these noncrying cues, he won't need to cry as much. He will have more time to practice and expand his non-crying sounds and imitate adult sounds. He will likely become more proficient in speech than a child who has to cry for everything he wants.

Most people mistakenly believe that the baby's only means of communication is crying. They *expect* him to cry, and, because they do not respond to his other methods of expression, he is forced to cry to get his needs attended to. But don't think he should never cry. Crying often provides exercise, and frequently relieves frustration. Excessive crying should always be investigated. But use common sense. He must learn that crying does not necessarily get him what he wants.

Because he is socially inclined, he should be where the activity is during his waking hours as long as that activity is not too noisy. By three or four months, he will have new ways to express his delight—laughing, squealing, cooing, and a variety of babbling sounds in imitation of what is said to him. He will like to have you repeat the sounds he makes back to him in a two-way conversation game. He likes adult talk too, and he absorbs more than you think. Don't toss him constant chatter but talk to him about his bath, food, and other routines as if he could understand everything. Use simple, short sentences, correct names for things, and clear, correct pronunciation. Sound practice here means much to his language development and later clear use of his mother tongue. He may babble more when alone than when with people. He needs this vocalizing practice also.

Pat-a-cake, peek-a-boo, and being carried around the room in mother's arms while she marches to good music are some favorite games for your baby's early months of life. He begins to see differences in faces, enough so that he may even act afraid or shy if a stranger comes too close. If he has security in consistent, loving parenting, however, he is usually able to respond confidently to others in a social way. But expect him to show preferences in people as well as in his activities.

Language and gestures are learned by imitation. So watch your example. While he is still practicing on syllables, baby will mimic your facial expressions, your tone of voice and inflections. Some of these he will double, like "da da" and "ma ma," perhaps because he finds they please dada and mama so much. He will copy your mannerisms, defects, or whatever good or bad characteristics you have. And even though the eight-month-old infant does not yet talk, this does not mean he doesn't understand—at least those things which pertain to him. He has come a long way in a short time.

Shortly, he will get much pleasure from naming things, matching words to objects and endlessly repeating them to reaffirm his newly gained knowledge and to build self-confidence. He will enjoy telling you, for example, what the various animals say. Don't be concerned if language development slows a bit during his big push to walk. Somehow one of these major hurdles is all he can handle at one time. So let him develop naturally at his own pace with encouragement and support but without pressure.

The Little Gymnast

Your baby is born with a good grasp reflex, holding his fists tightly clenched. That's why he will grab your fingers to pull up to a sitting position or hold a rattle for a while. At three or four months he will be reaching for things to grasp and put in his mouth. Practice in this routine makes him more skillful in his eye-hand coordination. He already has favorite things. But one item at a time is best. Often he is able to play with his hands or with just one toy for quite a long period of time. This helps to lengthen his attention span. A variety of toys or too many choices confuse him and interfere with his concentration.

By the end of four months he will have fairly steady control of his head and can turn it from side to side. He will also be able to roll over and sit, propped up with pillows or in a jumper seat where he can see what is going on. He can't really stand on his legs, but with help he surely will try, especially on your lap.

Baby's clothes should be loose and short enough to allow freedom of movement without his being chilled. His limbs should be kept as warm as his body. This insures unrestricted circulation of blood and the oxygen it carries to keep the cells healthy and strong. He likes to wave his arms and kick his feet. If you put his feet against a wall, he will push against it. At bathtime and just before bedtime he may have the opportunity of exercising without the restriction of clothes. Stretching and squirming may be mixed with giggles of glee. But be careful that he does not wriggle off the bed or table. A clean sheet or blanket on the floor is safer for baby's calisthenics. Encouraging "cheers" and a little back rub from the care-giver will help to spur him on in this very important motor development.

A playpen near the family activities is a clean, safe place for baby to perform his gymnastics. He will learn to entertain himself and be happy there for several short periods during the day if he starts young enough. It provides opportunities for his early practice in physical development—arching his back while on his tummy, rolling over, pulling himself up to a standing position and walking round and round with support. This gives him self-confidence and a certain independence.

The Explorer

When he can be watched carefully, give your baby the chance to explore. He has great curiosity and needs to find out all he can that is appropriate and safe. The physical exercise involved in crawling from room to room at around eight months helps him develop confidence, balance, coordination, and strength. He can soon shift from creeping to sitting to prone position. If he can have a cabinet or a box in the kitchen for his very own, you can more fairly and easily teach him to leave your cupboards and drawers alone—an early lesson in respect for others' property. His space can be stocked with a catalogue or magazine, pans with lids that fit, nested measuring cups, and boxes or other containers with lids. Breakable or dangerous articles in the house (this includes detergents and cleaning supplies) should be mostly removed from his reach to minimize accidents and "no-no's." Keep poisons locked away.

This is an important time to continue the discipline begun at birth. Remember that your baby is not able fully to reason or understand the why of an issue. He will not learn this consistently until after age seven. He must obey simply because you say so. Though the human baby is far superior to animals in potential, his training must be similar to animal training until his reasoning is developed. The ability to reason largely determines the difference between training and education. With patience, consistency, repetition, and approval for good behavior, the very young child can be trained to know what is acceptable and unacceptable behavior. As he grows older, he will gradually learn more of the "why" of things and will develop sound judgment.

At this point, it is a real advantage to the parent that the child can be easily distracted or diverted. Sometimes retrieving him when he does not come when called or removing him from the forbidden object with a very simple explanation of what you expect is a good technique. Yet at his age this sort of thing must be repeated often to get the point across. A little snap on an offending hand if it disregards your "no-no" may be necessary at times, but anything more severe is questionable. Be sure you are in control of your own emotions and never slap or impatiently scold. Such actions expose your lack of composure and control. Because his memory is short and his conscience is undeveloped, he is not safe out of your sight unless he is in his bed or playpen, and even there needs your occasional eye.

At this stage there are inevitable minor bumps and bruises. How the child responds to these will largely depend on you. If you take them seriously, he will also. If you are relaxed and relatively unconcerned, he will be, too. Sometimes he will momentarily size up his audience before deciding whether to laugh or cry.

New skill in coordination is achieved at about eight or nine months—pounding on something or banging two things together, transferring an item from one hand to the other, putting things into containers and placing rings on a stationary stick. Stacking blocks is too complicated for a while yet. Ordinary household items such as a plastic bucket and old-fashioned clothespins or empty spools to put in it can give practice in coordination. And your baby will enjoy small pans, cans, or cups which stack, and other safe plastic containers. All babies love a spoon and a pan, but to save the noise for the sake of your nerves and baby's ears, use a plastic or cardboard container and a wooden spoon.

The baby's senses of taste and smell are quite well developed from the very first, so when he is awake enough of the day to enjoy a tour around the house or outdoors he will like smelling flowers, perfume, or other interesting odors. Perhaps baby's mouth is more sensitive to textures than are his hands at first, but soon he can crumple a dry leaf or feel such things as bark, fur, different kinds of rocks, shells, sand, or cloth. Everything is a new experience and will provide all the excitement your fledgling child needs.

The Healthy Eater

The introduction of solid foods too early has been found to cause allergic reactions and may be responsible for overfeeding. So the baby's tasting of foods other than fruit juice should be delayed until he is four to eight months old, depending on your doctor's suggestion. How you manage his regular feeding schedule and the introduction of new foods will determine to a great extent his eating habits for life. Likes, dislikes, and other patterns of diet are not inherited; they are environmentally developed and they clearly affect his health, his self-control, and his mental ability. Your patience, understanding, consistency, and educated common sense, as well as your calm, unhurried attitude can make your child a good eater.

Any new food should be introduced when the baby is really hungry—not after filling him up with milk. And to begin with such new attempts should be limited to only once a day. It should be in very small quantities—not more than one or two teaspoons—and offered in tiny bites off the tip of a small spoon. If he should spit it out, it does not necessarily indicate that he doesn't like it. It may take him a number of tries to learn how to swallow solid foods efficiently. If he really seems not to like it, say nothing but discontinue it for a while. Bring it back considerably later in very small amounts when his appetite is good. If he likes it, offer the same food every day for a week or so until he gets used to it. It is best to start with something like scraped fresh apple, pureed applesauce without sugar, or mashed banana. But give only one type of solid food at a meal, along with his milk.

Babies are not ready for whole grain cereal or toast until they are more than six months old. When they begin to cut teeth and drool, you know that the salivary glands are producing *amylase,* which is necessary for the proper digestion of starchy foods and less finely strained fruits and vegetables.

At about this same time baby may be willing to omit his late evening feeding, although this may bring about an adjustment to an earlier feeding in the morning. Then gradually the interval between meals should be broadened until by the age of one year baby is on three regular meals with nothing but water between. Many mothers will be surprised at this suggestion, but it works well for normal babies and forms a foundation for healthy children. Snacks or even fruit juice between meals disturbs normal digestion, causing residue to be left in the stomach as long as thirteen hours or more, whereas the normal emptying time would be two and a half to four hours. During this delayed or partial digestion, toxic chemicals such as aldehydes, alcohols, and esters are produced, adversely affecting the brain, liver, kidneys, and other delicate tissues. This sets the stage for later digestive problems whose origins seem obscure or are blamed on other conditions.

We watched one noon as little Jackie Morton, age five, turned from his vegetables. For two reasons, we were curious about how his mother, Jeanne, would handle him. First, her three youngsters were among the best behaved children we had ever seen and, second, we knew Jackie's example was bound to be a signal to his

little brothers. We also knew that children's appetites are sometimes capricious. A youngster may come to a meal and not be
hungry—for any number of reasons: excitement, a bad day at
school, ridicule by neighbor kids, a slight fever, or even a secret
piece of candy between meals. Or often parents will fill their dishes
too full and youngsters stare in futility.

But Jeanne knew these sensible rules: never force, coax, nag,
bribe, or show undue concern. These simply make a poor eating
habit an attention-getting device. She knew Jackie was not likely
to starve. And if he were possibly ill, his stomach could do with a
rest.

She ran her fingers through the hair on his forehead, then said,
"You can run on up to your room and rest." Her tone was gentle
but firm. Jackie had made his pitch. If he were ill, bed was the best
place for him and she would be around to care; if not—well, he
had tested her and found her consistent and knew that he would
get nothing until supper. (We found out later that Jackie ate a
whopping meal that night.)

But what if you have not been so careful and consistent and your
children have fallen into bad eating and behavior habits? What if
you find you have been indifferent and then try to make it up by
being over-concerned the next time? Your child knows even as
early as eight to twelve months when he has you on such a roller
coaster. This is the time to reevaluate your own life style, tensions,
and irregularities, and appraise them against the worth of your
child. Don't be hesitant to ask for divine help, and set out to be
consistently warm and tender, but wisely firm. Your child will be
much more secure, and, like Jeanne's, a source of pride.

Were you wondering what Jeanne did that afternoon? She was
quite sure Jackie had no fever, but she took his temperature—a
gesture which was as significant to her son as it was informative to
her. And she did not give him anything but water between meals,
no matter how her tender spirit wished to do so, nor how loud his
stomach growled. If she had given in to his pleas, she would have
lost her self-respect and his regard as well and left him insecure and
misbehaved.

Be careful of overfeeding or allowing baby to become too chubby. This is at least as bad as undernourishment, because fat babies often become fat children who become fat maladjusted adults who cannot control their appetites. Such indulgence constitutes a serious health hazard. Fat cells formed in these early years make it difficult, if not impossible, to maintain normal weight in adulthood. Normally the baby should about double his birth weight by six months and possibly triple it by one year.

A good family example is one of baby's best teachers. If the mealtime atmosphere is pleasant, uncritical, uncomplaining, and cooperative, baby will follow suit. He will learn to like what is set before him. Natural, unprocessed foods that do not contain or have not been fried in such greases as margarine, butter, or mayonnaise and without sugar or very much salt are best for everyone. If tastes are trained in this way to begin with, much illness can be prevented. It is normal to have preferences and these can be honored within reason. Some families have a rule that everyone eats something of everything that is served, but a minimum of what is liked least. But do not rely on your child's natural inclination to be his nutritional guide. If you do, sweets and empty calories will soon be the order of the day, and you will have more troubles than you could have imagined.

Before the baby is a year old he can begin to feed himself, starting with finger foods like slices of banana, thin strips of Melba toast, well-cooked thin slices of carrot, whole cooked green beans, or wedges of a ripe apple. Even with only four to six teeth and good working gums he can pulverize these foods satisfactorily. Let him try spoon feeding, too. He will be messy, but plastic bibs and water are cheap compared to the value of self-reliance and responsibility you will want to develop in him. For the next year or two he will usually need help to finish his meal for he tires of the process.

Ease into teaching him to drink water, milk, and fruit juices from a cup as early as five or six months of age, only a sip at a time. When he does this well and can hold a cup, chews well and helps to feed himself, weaning may be introduced *gradually*. If he is breast-fed, he can be weaned from the breast to the table. It isn't wise to postpone this too long, for the process could become more difficult if delayed. Eating with the family should be encouraged as the growing up thing to do—another step toward independence. We do not propose here to set limits, for circumstances alter cases, but perhaps somewhere around a year or fourteen months for most mothers should be the end of the breast for the young child's meals.

The Little Worker

Although we will talk more about work in the next few pages, now is the time to get ready. As we suggested at the first of this chapter, working with you is a special happy time for your small child. You can start with a box in the corner of his crib and teach him to put his toys away before you pick him up. When he starts walking, have a box in the corner. Teach him to put his toys away before he goes shopping with you. It will take your special effort for a few weeks, but your patience and persistence here will pay off many times over. You will be much happier parents and have a self-respecting child—with toys out from underneath your feet and a child who has begun to learn character lessons of responsibility and neatness and order, and of partnership in the home.

CHAPTER SIX

The Winsome Ones and the Terrible Twos

Parents are strange creatures. Most want to have children, but after the newness has worn off, sometimes they aren't so sure. When their little ones are small and completely dependent, they are quite conscientious about good physical care. They even keep in close touch with their doctor or read books on child care. Excitedly they note and encourage every new achievement and ability. But after the babies' first year or so when they begin to get around for themselves, the parents often become less attentive to their needs. Sometimes they are quite unaware of some of their simplest requirements. They are like some teachers who pass some students by.

With your child's growing intelligence, physical mobility, and developing personality, he should have your attention as much as or more than ever. He needs your continuing careful supervision and an environment that will help him grow safely and healthfully in every respect. *This does not take any great skill or magic.* It certainly does not require a teaching certificate or a college degree. (A teaching credential does not guarantee the ability to teach a classroomful of students.) But it does require a dedication to the task of parenting. You are wise to learn from those more experienced or better trained in child development and rearing. Such homespun knowledge or professional help should be carefully compared, applied with common sense, and adapted to the particular needs of your children.

The ultimate goal of growing up is to attain a desirable independence. A child naturally reaches out for this individuality during every waking moment. The parents' responsibility is lovingly, delicately, gradually, and prayerfully to help him accomplish this. The wise, alert parent will watch for cues as to what the child is wanting or trying to do and will help or encourage him only as much as is necessary so that the child can happily grow. The wise parent will not do for the child things he can do or could learn to do for himself. But he should not be deserted or left without encouragement to handle the inevitable frustrations that are a consequence of his limited size and ability.

TLC (Tender, Loving Care)

One of the most vital needs of your child is continued warm, responsive, and consistent relationship with you. The tiny, helpless infant is irresistible to most adults, and tender, loving care comes easily. But as the child's will becomes stronger, his emotions burst out oftener and his need for independence is greater. He is no longer so cuddly and responsive. One friend who expected this to "last forever" found her child at age fifteen months to be "about as cuddly as a jack-rabbit." He was more interested in being on the move and into everything. Yet when you look fondly into his eyes, you find they are as naive and winsome as a bunny's.

The toddler still needs assurance of love in the tone of voice, in facial expressions, in words and in physical contact. As he receives love he is more able to give love. Children who have not received adequate affection grow up to live without it. A warm sense of security and belongingness is the most influential factor in the early socialization of the child and helps to determine how lovable and loving he will ultimately become.

Equally as important as the parents' love for their child is the parents' love for each other. If they show affection to one another and are happy together, the child will catch the spirit and learn to be a loving person. If he is a truly affectionate child, he is likely to become a happy and friendly adult. This leads eventually to better chances for satisfactory relationships in business, in marriage and in family life. It establishes a far-reaching and recurring cycle which helps to build or destroy society.

Training the Little Disciple

Neither indulgence nor overprotectiveness—"smother love"—is the genuine article. Both are basically selfish and do not consider the child's ultimate best good. The Bible stories of the sons of Aaron and Eliab and Eli and Samuel are tragic examples of such parental laxity. Genuine love involves a special kind of firmness, discipline, and mutual respect which organizes the child and lays the groundwork for future self-control. The best discipline is said to be the fine art of discipleship. Again the Scriptures give us poignant models: Rachel with Joseph and Benjamin; Mordecai with his niece, Esther; Zacharias and Elisabeth and their son, John; and Mary and Joseph and the Christ-child.

There is much evidence that parents of the brightest and best developed children are very loving but set definite limits. They have taken note that to be the best followers, their little disciples must have good leaders. Children are best taught by parental example. Work with them, play with them, eat with them, read with them, and when they rest—which should be plenty—you should rest, too, or catch up on those things which are most difficult with them around.

The better your control up to the first year, the less conflict there will be as your growing child learns to accept prohibitions. Make your rules few, but enforce them well. If you do not do this thoroughly now, it will be much more difficult later. As early as eight or nine months, your child not only can understand very well what you say to him, but he can also understand how definite, or indulgent, you are about what you say. He has you figured out before he reaches his first birthday.

You can make obedience a pleasure for your child by your

consistency, your loving firmness, and your manner. If possible, let him observe an animal family and watch how the mother cares for the babies and keeps them close to her. Show him pictures and tell him about some he may not be able to see firsthand and how the babies must obey. Emphasize the obedience of baby chicks, for instance, when the mother hen says, "Cluck, cluck," and they come running. Sometimes you can play "mother" animal, clucking, meowing, barking, or other sounds to call your "baby" animal, and he can come running and answer as the little creature would do.

You must also offer courtesy and consideration. For example, when you must interrupt his activity, give him a little warning, such as, "When that stack of blocks falls down, please come to lunch," or, "You may jump off the step one more time before we go in." The worst thing you can do is to be inconsistent, allowing a certain behavior one time, but punishing it another time, or insisting that he finish all his vegetables before he eats his dessert, and then failing to follow through. Firmness and consistency in a cheerful, settled, and loving manner is the key. Parents should not apologize about cultivating, even praying for, such dispositions.

Disagreement between parents about the methods of child training or discipline is also very devastating to the child. Privately and frankly discuss any differences in your feelings about bringing up children and work out a solution or at least a truce so that the child does not become confused and fearful.

The Little Rebel

When their toddler is about two years old, parents often think they have a negative child. His almost constant response of "no" and other rather normal characteristics have brought on the label "Terrible Twos" for this age. Actually, he is not so negative as he is positive about asserting his independence. He is developing his own personality. Just meet him on his own terms, respect his need for individuality, use a little more wisdom than he has, and you will stay ahead of him. If there is no choice involved, don't ask him to make one. What child would normally answer "yes" if you asked him if he wants to go to bed? Or wash his hands for lunch? So don't ask him; simply proceed with the bedtime or washing routine.

If you don't want a negative response, it is best not to ask your child any questions or make any requests which could be readily answered by "no." Rather, make simple, kind statements about what is to be done, keeping him well informed, but not consulting his preferences until he gets past this stage, for example: "I am putting on my coat to go to the store. Here is your coat." In case after mealtime you wish to break the monotony, you might try asking him if he wants one of his favorite treats. He may even break over and say "yes." We hope this is an unsweetened treat such as fruit or a popsicle made with juice or yogurt. But be sure that it comes with a meal rather than between meals. To illustrate how children's tastes can be educated, our youngsters' favorite treats were brewer's yeast tablets! To them they were candy.

There are situations in which a choice between two acceptable alternatives helps to avoid a negative reaction. Instead of asking, "Do you want some peas?" ask, "Do you want your peas in a green dish or a yellow dish?" Or, "Shall we read the animal book or the growing-up book?" Also ask him lots of questions which require other types of answers, such as, "What does the duck say?" or, "Where does the rain come from?" An acceptable use of "no" might help to satisfy part of his special urge, as in the questions "Is the dog green?" or, "Does the frog say 'meow'?" And singing requests sometimes work like a charm when ordinary appeals would receive a negative reaction, especially if words like "Let's go" or "Let's do" are used.

The Crybaby and the Tantrum Child

A crybaby is one who has learned that crying is the surest way to get what he wants. If this is the case with your child, we hope it occurs to you that this will cause both him and you nothing but trouble from here on out. The only cure is never to give him what he wants, not even attention, when he cries. The exception, of course, is the occasion when you are sure he is sick or hurt—when your love will give him fullest attention. But be sure he gets lots of warmth and the right kind of attention when he is not crying. Listen carefully for the false cry or whine that turns off as fast as it turns on. Consistency is absolutely essential.

When crying becomes screaming, kicking, or writhing on the floor, it's a full-fledged temper tantrum. Again, prevention is simpler than cure. The measures are relatively simple. We also mention them in relation to child training in other sections of this book. Briefly, they go like this:

1. Maintain a quiet, simple environment and regular schedule for your family. Fatigue and noise, including loud music and confusion, make everyone's temper short. Irregular meals and between-meal snacks upset the stomach . . . and the disposition.

2. Allow your child reasonable freedom to explore in the house. Make sure there are relatively few, if any, forbidden items within his reach. These ground rules must be established from the beginning and consistently enforced by *both* parents.

3. Have plenty of opportunity for physical exercise outdoors to absorb excess energy and work off frustration.

4. Try to avoid head-on conflict by being tactful and kind, usually by distracting the child.

5. Never show anger in dealing with your child, in word, action—e.g., shoving, kicking or slapping—or by your tone of voice.

Some children will have tantrums nevertheless. We suspect that if parents were perfect, children would more likely be perfect. But sometimes we have to make corrections in our children to accommodate our lack of patience or consistency. In any case, it is imperative that you subdue his very first display of temper. If you do not, each instance will be more violent and more difficult to cure. Do not allow your child to get his own way by this means. You cannot afford to make a single exception to this rule, even if the tantrum puts you in an embarrassing position such as in the supermarket or at church. In this case, you can pick him up bodily to take him where you can eventually get his tantrum under control, but don't give in. Here are some suggestions on control:

1. An effective technique for the infant or very small child is to hold him very firmly, at the same time talking quietly or singing in his ear.

2. As a distraction—not a bribe—this same method may work for an older child if you catch him just as he starts.

3. Otherwise, calmly *ignore* him the best you can, for it is attention to his anger that he wants. Spanking, scolding, or anger on your part is not appropriate.

4. When his temper subsides, show your love by holding him and telling him how sorry you are that he got so upset about such a little thing. Elicit his assurance that he will try not to do that anymore. You might even tell him a little story about how someone you knew acted that way, but learned to do better. Then promptly go on to something else pleasant and active as if the incident had never happened. Give him a job to do with you that you know he likes.

Whether the problem is tantrums, unnecessary crying, disobedience, or simple indifference, a wise parent recognizes it as selfishness, which means that the child is putting himself ahead of you or is bothering others. So you may have to isolate him as Jeanne Morton did Jackie.

But remember, she did not reject him! When he came downstairs after lunch, she asked, "Well, who do we have here?"

He looked at her sheepishly.

"Are you feeling okay?" Again she flipped up the tousled hair of his forehead.

When he answered, "Yah," she smiled, tweaked his nose, and turned back to the sink. The matter was settled and he knew it. He was secure.

When our Dennis or Kathie cried unnecessarily Dorothy would often say, "Oooh, your crying hurts my ears, so please go to your room."

"But Mama," Kathie would say, "I don't want to."

"But this isn't a crying room," Dorothy would answer. "We'll see you when you are through."

Kathie knew that her mother meant what she said. When she returned, Dorothy would always give her a quick, but not overindulgent, hug or kiss and change the pace by suggesting some happy activity they could do together. This was not a time for Kathie to be sent out to play by herself and possibly feel rejected.

Blueprints for Eating

After the first year there is a reduction in your child's appetite as his growth rate slows down. He is probably the best judge of how *little* he can eat, but not always how much or what. He does not have the judgment to choose his own foods unless it is a choice between two equally acceptable alternatives. Until he can learn the principles of nutrition and is capable of applying them, you must decide what foods he should eat, with reasonable allowance for food preferences.

Offering sweets or dessert as a bribe for eating other food is bad practice. This attaches some special value to such food and encourages overeating, and often becomes an almost unsolvable problem later on. We feel that permissiveness or mishandling of a child's eating habits is a form of child abuse because it has such far-reaching results. Even wasting food might be better than offering bribes, but there is a more satisfactory method of establishing good eating patterns.

First, avoid any eating between meals. A child cannot really appreciate and enjoy food if he is never allowed to get hungry. Snacking, a damaging American pastime, keeps the digestive system continually at work, tearing down the efficiency of the whole body. All parts of the body including the organs of digestion require periods of activity followed by periods of rest. For example, the salivary glands contain enzymes which are released into the mouth when food is chewed. At the end of the meal these enzymes are relatively depleted. However, after three or four hours they have been replenished in readiness for another meal. A similar process goes on with the bile from the liver and the juices of the stomach, intestines, and pancreas, all of which aid in digestion. In other words, the whole cycle is set up to handle regular meals, preferably five hours or so apart, to allow for work and rest. If a new food is eaten which interrupts this cycle, the secretions are not sufficient to work properly. This causes delayed digestion, fermentation, and abuse of the digestive system, and it multiplies the normal digestive time. Unnecessary accumulation of wastes in the colon often brings constipation and opens the way for disease. When behavior or emotional problems then result in the child, few understand that they were brought on by irregular eating.

Second, start with *very small* helpings of balanced, healthful food. When all this is finished, the child may be given second helpings of something he prefers. This avoids a common problem of the child filling up on bread or milk or both and leaving his other food to be scraped into the garbage can. Generally, children like simple, unmixed foods, neither too hot nor too cold.

Third, wherever in a meal your child stalls or starts to dawdle, taste the food to see that it is not spoiled or inedible for some reason. Don't be concerned if it is not salty or sweet enough for your taste. If it is good, offer one more bite with encouraging approval of its taste. The child may simply be tired and need help to finish. Perhaps he has been given too much food to begin with or is not really hungry. In case of refusal, calmly excuse him from the table and allow nothing except water until the next meal. This kind of training will test your self-control, but it pays very well. Refrigerate the food and then present it again at the next meal. You may or may not warm it, according to your discretion, but never discard it unless it is spoiled. It is no more soggy or messy at the next meal than it was while he was dawdling. Generally, one or two experiences like this will take care of the matter unless you have already established poor eating habits.

In our counseling, where parents have faithfully followed this procedure, we cannot recall a single failure. In fact, there are hospitals that treat cases of extreme eating problems in this same manner. Some children may refuse several meals before they become hungry enough to eat what is set before them. One of the firm requirements of the program is to educate the parents to discard their former methods and adopt this simple technique, so that the old habits will not be allowed to resurface when the child returns home.

Some children seem to have enormous appetites and a tendency toward fatness. They need to be kindly and gently restrained until they have acquired enough reasoning ability, self-control, and understanding of nutrition to monitor themselves. Obesity is not only a health problem but is often a social, emotional and serious psychological problem to the child. Prevention is the best way to avoid a lifelong struggle against excess weight. If there is a tendency toward this in the family, a change in the diet and general life style of all will be beneficial. Too many refined, starchy, fatty and sweet foods, between-meal snacks, and lack of exercise are the main causes. These excesses lead to heart problems, diabetes and other debilitating diseases.

Because fatness can become such a serious disadvantage to the child, parents should make every effort to train the appetite carefully from birth. It is so much easier to begin right. Your baby's tastes are not yet perverted by sugar on his cereal, mayonnaise on his salad, butter on his bread, and salt on his food. We have a young, buoyantly healthy college friend who was brought up on simple, natural foods, and we have always envied her unperverted tastes as we struggle to retrain ours to a more healthful way! She has been a good example to us and strong evidence of the value of early training of the appetite.

Every effort should be made for the family to have at least one unhurried meal together each day. We always tried to have at least two. Mealtime should be a happy togetherness time. Conversation about other pleasant topics besides food should dominate. If all eat with joy and thankfulness, the newest family member will develop the same positive attitudes. And don't forget the "grace" for your meals—the thankful request for God's blessing on the food and the hands that prepared it and those who will be nourished. Even when eating out, it is very special to see a family that is not shy about thanking their God.

Building In Health and Safety Features

The quality of air in the home is important to the child's health. Until he is eight to ten years old he will be more susceptible to respiratory infections than he will be after that age. If family members smoke in the home, he will have at least twice the difficulty with this problem as in a smoke-free environment. If he is asthmatic or allergic to tobacco smoke, it may be even more harmful to him. Some researchers now believe that second-hand fumes breathed in by the nonsmoker may be even more dangerous than to the smoker himself.

Outdoor work and play involves health as well as development of large muscles. Vigorous exercise helps the blood circulate and requires deep breathing, both of which are vital for nourishing the body, and thus the brain, with oxygen. It also aids digestion, makes one thirsty and stimulates growth and coordination of the muscles. The sunshine absorbed provides natural vitamin D, kills germs, and probably contains some valuable life-giving qualities not yet fully understood by science. Even on cold or rainy days, children should be dressed appropriately and allowed to play or work a reasonable time out of doors.

The freedom to explore at this age is crucial to the development of creativity and intelligence, but help him satisfy his curiosity about the world without letting him out of your sight. Take care; he will not only look and touch, but he will lick, squeeze, pound, throw, and swallow. He has no idea about danger. Accidents are the leading cause of death in young children. They bring more injuries and deaths than the leading six childhood diseases combined. For example, one-fifth of all poisonings take place at this age. We repeat our caution that you put out of reach or lock up all cleaning items, insecticides, or anything dangerous that he could drink or eat. And don't leave one out on the drainboard while you answer the doorbell or telephone.

When you think of how terrible some of these things would taste to you, remember that his taste is not selective and even a small amount can cause serious illness or death. Watch out for lamp cords, electric sockets, fireplaces, pins, scissors, knives and pans with handles which protrude over the edge of the stove or sink. Think ahead as you put a constant watch on small objects which can cause choking or lung damage. Even nuts, tiny hard candies, or popcorn can be dangerous. Put safety gates on stairs, and protective covers on unused electrical outlets. Remember, your child is not a little adult!

If you allow your little one a little pre-bath water play in the tub, DON'T LEAVE HIM ALONE EVEN FOR A MOMENT. Bring your knitting, mending, or even a book while keeping watch. And if the doorbell or telephone rings, and you must answer it, wrap him in a towel and TAKE HIM WITH YOU. You may be compelled to ignore the phone, but DON'T IGNORE HIM.

Your Child's Worth as a Worker

An evaluation of his own worth is a subconscious learning of the young child. He achieves this in large part by the way he thinks others value him. And the foundation is laid in his family. If he is loved, positively disciplined, and encouraged in his abilities and desire to be independent, he will have a good self-concept. But if his parents act as though he is an irritation and a problem to them, he will accept their point of view as correct. In fact, over-busy or distracted parents can easily give the child the impression that he is in the way.

A very important way for him to build his concept of self-worth is to make him a valued and desired part of the family team. As soon as he is able to walk, he can start to put his toys away with help and encouragement from mother or daddy. Make it a game: "Let's make the toys jump into the box." Work should not be so much a matter of obeying orders or requests as it should be a cooperative effort for the good of all—the pleasure of a neat, orderly home. The child should be made to feel that his work is needed and appreciated. The right attitude is essential here.

It would, of course, really be easier at first for you to do everything yourself. Yet you should let your little one start when he is willing though not very able if you want him to still be willing when he is more able. Let him wash his hands, feet, and knees at bath time. He'll learn that they come in pairs. Soon he can "help" set or clear the table, make the beds, do simple errands, empty the trash, "dust" the furniture, and "wash" the floor, or clean the car wheels or bumpers while daddy is washing the car. His efficiency will be less than desirable but should be valued and complimented.

Remember, start these constructive chores when your child starts to walk. *Let him know early that he lives to be useful and to help you and others, not simply to be entertained!* Don't give him a job by himself and then do it over in front of him to show your superior skill. Instead, do it with him, patiently teaching him and making up the difference between his best effort and your standard without belittling his part. His skill will improve with practice, and you will find him to be a dependable partner in a few short months and years.

The Little Speech-Maker

At the beginning of this age period, the child's language consists of only a few words. Most of them are names of things. He adds new ones rapidly and enjoys reciting them for your approval and entertainment. If he hears good conversation and has opportunities to practice his abilities he will proceed toward relatively fluent speech by age three. It should be carefully noted that television talk is not effective in providing these experiences. Television supplies little or no opportunity for essential repetition or response, and therefore it is not helpful in language development. It may even have a negative effect because the child often tunes out TV's incessant machinelike chatter and noise.

The small child will talk a lot to himself. This typical

characteristic of early speech is valuable in helping the child sort out and organize his thoughts. His speech will also reflect his social progress, which at this point is still relatively self-centered. He will talk mostly about himself and things around him. You can guide him into more socialized speech mostly by your example, by giving him plenty of opportunity to help in the home, and by refusing to focus a lot of inappropriate attention on his cuteness and brightness.

Because speech is so largely learned by imitation, you will need to take special care to provide good models for him to copy. The language patterns you present will probably be carried by your child through life. Each of us who write this book had little trouble with grammar classes in school. The language examples provided us in our homes saved us a great deal of later anguish and frustration. This is a significant way you can make your youngsters' eventual school life happier and more productive. Bad grammar, faulty pronunciation, and poor enunciation are difficult to correct in later years even with diligent instruction and perseverance. You may feel that using the child's kind of speech in talking to him will enable him to understand you better. This does not happen. He understands a great deal more than he is able to express, but he cannot do much to improve his language if you are imitating him.

Toilet Matters

As in eating, sleeping, and any kind of development, the use of force will not bring the desired result in toilet training. Attempting training too early or with pressure may even have long-term negative consequences. Do all you can to insure your child's cooperation by making it attractive or profitable to do so. Patience and consistent but not extravagant praise will be your best allies. Fortunately, he has a built-in desire for your approval, and if this motivation has not been squelched by improper treatment, it will help you immensely in the management of this rather sensitive step forward. He also is eager to achieve independence—to grow up. Don't ever shame or depreciate him or show disdain for his current habits. Most children are not greatly disturbed by wet, messy, or bulky diapers. By all means, in toilet training or in any other development, don't compete with your friends or compare your child with the neighbor's children. Each child is different from every other, and there may be as much as three or four years' difference in the maturity of children of a given age under ten or twelve. However, there is a readiness for each progressive step and the parent should be alert to the signals.

Bowel training comes first, but only with certain physical and mental maturities. Successful training involves the ability to stop a natural release, hold it, and then let it go at a particular place and time. The muscles should be sufficiently ready for this somewhere around a year or more, generally after your child learns to walk. And he needs to be able to communicate his need by word, sound, or action.

This is where regularity begins to show its shining best. If your child is on a systematic program and has had an early morning drink of warm water a half hour or more before breakfast and if his diet is of unrefined, natural foods with plenty of fresh fruit and vegetables, he will probably have a regular bowel movement right after breakfast. If you can be casual—and not show disappointment or distress when he does not respond—you can place him on the potty for a few minutes at this time—seldom longer than five. The simplest device from your point of view is a potty seat placed on the regular toilet. If you handle this right, your child will not be afraid of it. If there is fear, you will have to settle for a child's potty chair which is less threatening than the higher commode. Some parents make a little stairway up to the toilet. This also gives him some security when his feet don't have to dangle. Make a happy little game of encouraging his efforts. Then compliment his success, but show love and pleasantness even without it. He will soon get the message and try to please you. As soon as reasonable results are evident, his motivation will be increased by his own sense of achievement.

There are some cases where the baby's schedule and diet are so very careful and regular that the bowel movement can almost be timed by the clock. Mother can be sure to use a disposable diaper for this or put him on the potty when he is able to sit up alone. In this way mother quite consistently avoids messy diapers, but the baby is not really trained in the full sense of the word. If there is a change in the program, he may forget he ever did it.

The next step, at around eighteen months or later, is daytime bladder control. Here girls begin to show up the boys in maturity. They are generally ready as much as six months earlier than boys. It is often easier to accomplish bladder training in hot weather when clothes are brief and perspiration is an ally. When your baby awakes from a nap with a dry diaper, put him on the potty a few moments. Tell him the best you can what to do. Running the water in the lavatory a moment or putting the child's hands in warm water may help to trigger a reaction. If so, give approval. If not, hug him anyway. And never mind if he immediately wets the dry diaper you put on him. Then start taking him to the bathroom the first thing in the morning, before or after meals, before or after naptime, before bedtime, and before leaving the house. This should be quite consistent, but we are dubious about an all-out campaign like a three-day or one-week training course, although we admit it will work in some cases. Don't risk your child's resentment by unnecessarily interrupting his work or play activities; don't overdo it, and don't argue about it. Soon he will have a few dry days—then stay quite consistently dry—girls generally about two and a half, boys by about age three.

Occasional relapses are normal. A change in circumstances may unsettle him for weeks, but these should be taken in stride. If you run into any serious troubles, back off for awhile and analyze your situation. Perhaps you started too soon, put on too much pressure, or tried too hard. Then after a time, start over with calmness, assurance, love, encouragement, and consistency . . . and if you are brave enough, by example.

Night-dryness comes next and, in terms of age, might better belong in the next chapter. But for consistency we will include it in its sequence for this kind of training. When your child wakes up dry in the morning, applaud him and encourage him. If you concentrate on liquids early in the day and minimize them late in the day, it will be easier. But don't let this become an issue. Don't make it a punishment or deprivation. You may gradually be able to explain to your child the connection between drinks and a full bladder. Also take him to the bathroom once or twice during the night—when you go to bed and once more. If you find him already wet, take him earlier next time. Some people feel that waking the child completely each time so he knows what he is doing helps him to learn more quickly to go to the bathroom by himself when he gets a signal that his bladder needs to be emptied. Occasional night wetting is to be expected in a child under four years. Any consistent relapses after this are probably due to some underlying emotional insecurity or disturbance. In this case, the cause has to be determined and remedied, if possible. There are sometimes physical causes but these are infrequent.

The Dawdler

Dawdling is a two-year-old characteristic which is often frustrating to a parent. Your child has no appreciation of time except for *now*. He is not easily hurried or delayed. His patience is short. He usually wants what he wants when he wants it. Paradoxically, he may spend long periods clasping, manipulating, banging, and intently studying something which fascinates him. If reasonable, do not disturb this type of soliloquy. It not only helps to develop muscular coordination, increasing your child's skill and speed of movement, but it also lengthens his attention span and increases his concentration.

We remember well our little perfectionist son. He learned well to put everything away perfectly. His room was a model of tidiness. But, oh, the price we paid in his exasperating slowness. We called him "the cow's tail." He thought that was funny. It in no way damaged his little ego.

As we look back we see that we did not handle this problem

effectively. During his school days we often waited in the car for him when we should have left him home by himself to learn a lesson which he had later to learn more painfully.

A two or three-year-old can be tempted with the hope of going to the store or the park with mommie or daddy, and with some consistency, will learn to move faster than a turtle. He is not very efficient as he tries to do things for himself. Yet his efforts to do it "all by myself" are a commendable part of becoming independent. As much as possible, he should be allowed to do this even if he gets his shoes on the wrong feet and his undershirt back-side front. If there is a deadline to meet, try to start him enough ahead of time so he will be ready in time without nagging or scolding. A helpful device we used for this and other activities which need some limitation was an automatic timer set for a reasonable completion time. An alarm clock will do if a timer is not available. This eliminates the personal element involved in enforcement; rather, the ringing of the buzzer or bell is the authoritative signal. The child will soon take great fun in trying to finish before the bell.

The Security Force

If the home program has been regular, the two-and-a-half-year-old finds great satisfaction and stability in doing the same things the same way day after day. He is a creature of routine; in fact, he is downright ritualistic. He is happy in knowing what to expect, and he will be very insecure if his life is not on a reasonably regular schedule. This natural desire for order and routine as well as his effort to become independent are key characteristics on which you can capitalize.

Now is the time to teach him to keep his room, closet, and dresser drawers neat, to put away groceries, and to help keep everything in its place. Chalk outlines of certain toys can be made on a shelf or the floor to show the correct places—a "garage" for the truck, a "hangar" for the airplane. Provide shelves, hooks, nails, or rods at his height so that he can do all that is possible to help himself. Mount a mirror at his eye level. If possible, make or buy a child-size table and chair, or use a strong wooden box or other work place his size. Also, as much as possible provide clothes with front zippers, large buttons, and other self-help gadgets. We believe our son's preciseness and methodical habits largely established at this age have contributed to his ability as a researcher.

Your toddler likes occasional surprises but not in the way of unexpected visitors, trips, a new babysitter, a visit to the doctor or dentist or a house move. They are at best unwelcome and at worst may trigger panic. Preparation ahead of time is imperative if you want him to react in a reasonable manner. Explain simply and cheerfully what will probably happen and what you expect him to do. He may not understand fully and consistently, but he deserves your thoughtfulness. In some cases, you should role-play the situation to better prepare him for the event. Pretend that you are the dentist, for example, and demonstrate what the dentist does in inspecting his teeth. Or pretend to be the visitor and help your child learn how to be a good host or hostess. These are incidental opportunities to teach manners and other social graces by precept and example.

The Player . . . or the Worker

Play is a vital learning medium for a child. In a sense play is his work. He enjoys play and work equally until someone disillusions him with a negative attitude toward the latter. He learns to play as soon as he can see something or someone to play with. And he discovers knowledge for himself that cannot easily otherwise be taught. Through his senses and his manipulation of ordinary objects, he finds out about certain qualities of things—weight, textures, size, shape, and colors—the basis of academic learning. Through interaction with and observation and imitation of those around him he learns about life—the social skills. Through simple everyday activities and experiences he gradually develops basic concepts of time, number, and space. This continues through his first nine or ten years.

He really could get along without any commercial toys at all.

There are so many new and interesting things around—pans, spoons, spools, nested measuring cups for him to fit together, and all kinds of containers, as well as outdoor things to investigate. He will surprise you by his occasional long involvement with something which attracts him. These objects provide problem-solving situations for him which stimulate his thinking and help lengthen his attention span.

An example of the mental processes involved in playing with water would include discovering that water is easy to spill and hard to carry, that deep containers hold water better than shallow ones, that a sponge or towel will soak up water, that water runs out of a container if it has holes in it, that some things will float but some will sink, and that it takes many cups of water to fill up a bucket or big bottle. Later, at play or at work with you, he will learn just how many cups it takes to fill a pint or a quart or how many quarts to a gallon. As he arranges, handles, and compares other items he also learns their peculiar properties—things we have learned so long ago that we simply take them for granted.

A child can also be taught property rights at an early age. He should not be allowed to use any and all household objects as playthings. Whatever is specified as his should be in a particular place he can call his own, even if it's only a box in the corner. Shelves are better than a box for teaching neatness, but a box with only a few items in it is better than nothing. Having his special place encourages organization as well as establishes his right of ownership and sets limits on what he is allowed to use freely. It reinforces his security and self-worth.

This little verse can help to impress the fact that certain things belong to other members of the family. It can be sung to the tune of "Here We Go Round the Mulberry Bush" or the verse part of "Jesus Loves Me":

> This is mother's (daddy's), I won't touch
> For I love her (him) very much.
> I won't fuss and I won't whine
> I will play with what is mine.

Toys should be few and durable. Playthings that are easily broken teach destructiveness. Both boys and girls like the same kind of toys at this stage, things that they can make do something—push or pull toys that make noise, a small wagon, a tricycle, simple puzzles.

We have seen various kinds of light plastic balls a little larger than a Ping-Pong ball which have a special fascination for children in this age group. When bounced on an uncarpeted floor this ball produces fascinating sounds and movements, yet it is light enough and safe enough to be played with in the house. Just be sure the surface of the toy stays smooth and unbroken so as to avoid unnecessary cuts or scratches. Other small plastic containers may do as well for the throwing and chasing type of play which enhances baby's muscular coordination. He will also like large bean bags of sturdy, very firmly stitched material for stacking, playing catch, or throwing into a container. Check the fabric and the stitching before allowing the child to play with bags stuffed with beans or other small items that could be dangerous if they spilled out of a split seam or tear. We know of a child who choked to death in a freak accident of this kind.

Playthings that stir the imagination should have first priority. And we reemphasize, they don't necessarily have to be purchased toys. In fact, if a child had no store-bought toys at all, he would still have plenty of playthings. Everything he really needs is close at hand. Because this age child likes pull toys, let him help you tie a string on a small cardboard or wooden box, so he can pull it like a wagon. It can haul blocks, a stuffed toy, or doll. Blocks to build a tower, house, fence, or train can be made of smoothed wood scraps or even empty half-gallon milk cartons. The creative possibilities of a sandbox are unlimited if a few smooth, safe cans, a discarded strainer, a toy truck or two and a shovel or large spoon can be supplied. Digging tunnels, making hills and roads, or filling and emptying containers constitute profitable occupation for a toddler. On warm days, he could also have a small tub or bucket of water. This is the type of play which can and should occupy your child independently some of the time.

Other simple common items your child will enjoy are discarded greeting cards, a catalogue, or an old alarm clock with an unbreakable face; but don't give them to him all at once. For bad weather, equipment on a porch, or in the garage or in the basement will give him needed exercise, under supervision. These can be strong wood or cardboard boxes fastened together to climb on, an old mattress to jump or turn somersaults on and a small ladder laid down for him to walk between the rungs. If the ladder can be secured safely, it may be used for climbing.

One of the usual problems about toys is that there are too many of them. They are difficult to keep in order and the child is faced with too many choices. This is confusing to him and can be more of a hindrance than a help. If friends and grandparents have shown their love to your child by giving him or her many toys, put most of them away. Then bring them out one or two at a time to replace a currently used toy. By all means, don't frustrate or overwhelm your child with toys that are too advanced. Such things as kites, fancy dress-up dolls, or an electric train should be delayed until much later.

Summing Up

It is awesome to realize that even before he is three years old, your child has accomplished so much and virtually laid the base for all phases of his future life. Psychologists generally agree that the life-style, personality, language ability, mental potential, self-concept, attitude toward authority, and physical base are all pretty well set by the age of three. Although it is not absolutely essential to delay your next baby, a child has a special advantage in achieving the most in each of these areas if he can have these three years in a consistent relationship with his parents without the interruption of a new little brother or sister.

CHAPTER SEVEN

The Exploring Threes and Fours

Patty Spielman always viewed her granddaughter Patricia, nearly four, as a miniature adult. Indeed, her little namesake was very bright, and Mrs. Spielman was supremely convinced of her maturity until one day when "Pisha" was spending a few hours in her Newport Beach, California, apartment. Things had become quiet when Grandma became aware that again and again she was hearing the sound of rushing water. Realizing that the only other person around was little Patricia, Grandma quietly sauntered toward the bathroom expecting to see the tiny one intrigued with swirling toilet tissue or possibly potty-training her Barbie doll. Like any wise and well-mannered parent, she decided to be totally deliberate, gentle, and mature herself in handling this "situation."

Meanwhile, the flushing sounded anew. But little Pisha was occupied with neither toilet paper nor her doll. She had Grandmother's open purse and, one by one, was systematically flushing hundred-dollar bills down the commode. Stripped of her composure, Grandma Patty dived for the toilet bowl and grabbed the last of the paper currency floating its expensive circular path toward the drain.

"What on earth are you doing?" the astonished grandmother cried.

The little girl could not answer. She was too shocked at Grandma's antics, wondering only why on earth *she* was so disturbed.

Quickly retrieving her purse, her composure, and the remaining bills from Pisha's little fists, Mrs. Spielman began again to ask questions.

"Why are you flushing Grandma's money down the toilet?"

"Momma says money is 'icky'," Pisha stoically replied.

"But—" Then suddenly Patty Spielman cut herself short, realizing that there was at this point no reasonable "but" for a child not yet four. No matter how bright the little girl, there are some values and judgment levels which require time to mature. A child of four is simply not consistently reasonable. Patty Spielman knew instinctively that her granddaughter needed time to grow.

We have no record that children were created to be little imps. They generally learn what we teach them, or let them be taught. And therein lie many risks. The Bible tells us they were intended to be a blessing to parents, though there are bound to be problems. When we perceive them as children and teach them to be helpful, obedient, and pleasant, they are more joys than burdens.

Parents who understand this possibility are less inclined to let their youngsters run unsupervised with the neighborhood children or to allow them to watch television, or to be so glad to get them out from under foot that they will send them to school as early as possible. Whether their children's obnoxious behavior results from their own ignorance, indifference or incompetence, it is little wonder that some parents welcome nursery schools, summer day camps or whatever is available to give themselves a rest even at the risk of the children's failure. Such behavior is for the most part preventable or with sound information can to a large degree be remedied.

Building a Sound Body

Though all phases of a child's development are important, perhaps health—physical and mental—is the most important, for upon it all other development depends. A city apartment with television and without a play yard sets the stage for inadequate exercise for young children. Such a situation actually begs for degenerative diseases which are becoming more common in young children. Limiting or dispensing with television is a relatively simple preventive, but creating opportunities for vigorous physical activity will usually take greater parental effort and imagination. At this age the child needs several hours of physical activity a day. This helps to build the body, purify the blood, promote good digestion, and calm the nerves. Try to find a porch, backyard, vacant lot or park where he can climb, run, play, and work out of doors in the sunshine and fresh air as much as possible. Even in cold weather, dress yourself and him warmly and breathe deeply.

Daily bathing, clean clothes, and clean homes help to prevent illness and promote health. Outdoor play and work which inevitably get children dirty do not necessarily bring filth; gardening, sand-box play, or even making mud pies might be called "clean" dirt. It is the secretions from the body and the dirt from the streets which especially need regular removal.

Cleansing the body internally is equally important. Fruit juice or the water in our foods does not adequately replace plain, clear water. Children should be taught early to enjoy drinking plentiful amounts of water, never with meals but often between meals, beginning a half hour or more before breakfast. Water at mealtime dilutes the gastric juices and slows digestion. A drink of cool water—not cold—is the best method of staving off hunger until meal time, since it depresses the activity of the digestive system. The first-thing-in-the-morning drink—preferably warm—flushes out the kidneys, prepares the stomach for food by stimulating the glands on its walls, and helps the bowels move regularly and naturally. This ritual has been a real lifesaver for many families, usually making illness minor and rare.

Very cold, or very hot drinks are not usually good for the digestive system at any time. When they vary too greatly from body temperatures, they may cause shock to the system. Dentists warn against very cold food or liquids on the teeth. Physicians note that those who are habituated to very hot drinks are more likely to develop throat cancer and digestive difficulties.

If your child is not a good breakfast eater, don't say he inherited it from his mother or daddy. Good breakfast eaters are made, not born. He may be eating too heavy a meal too late in the evening. By heavy we mean vegetables and protein. A light meal of fruit and whole wheat toast at least two or three hours before bedtime will give the stomach better rest while the remainder of the body rests. Another reason may be that breakfast is introduced when he is too sleepy—either from too little or poor quality sleep—or too soon after getting up. If he has a glass of water upon awakening, with breakfast a half hour or more later, he will be more ready for food.

The concept of growing is not very easy for a young child to understand. You can help him by having him watch little animals, little plants, or other little creatures grow up. He can discover that it takes time to grow. Another device is to have a growth chart or a place to mark his growth on a door jamb or other inconspicuous place.

That Important Naptime

Parents of children in this age group often allow them to give up their naps. The reasons are common. Naps become too much of a hassle, or the children sleep too long in the afternoon and can't go to sleep at night. Sometimes parents would rather have them so tired that they hope to be able to get them to bed early and have them out of the way before the babysitter arrives or in time for a little peace and quiet. These may be valid enough reasons, but they do not consider the child's real needs. There is both research and clinical evidence that children who do not either nap or have at least an hour of very quiet rest time during the day are not able to get to sleep as well at night. Because they are overtired, they do not sleep as well when they do get to sleep. They are restless and more susceptible to bad dreams. This poor quality of nighttime sleep makes them vulnerable to fatigue again the next day. A vicious cycle is established, and then parents wonder why the children are excitable, irritable, hyperactive, and difficult to handle.

Our children were good nappers because there was never any question about whether or not they were going to sleep. Also, they soon discovered that getting to stay up longer or even go someplace in the early evening was adequate reward for the regular nap. One or two consistent experiences of being deprived of this privilege— the routine consequence of no nap—helped them understand the cause-and-effect relationship. Physical punishment or scolding in such cases is neither productive nor necessary.

I remember Dorothy telling four-year-old Dennis it was naptime.

"But," he would protest, "other kids don't have to take naps."

"And," she would answer, "some of the children are not as healthy as you." This was true, for he was robust, secure, and quite settled. But that point would make little impression on his yet immature reasoning ability.

So she would add, twinkling, "I'll let you get up if you keep your eyes closed without a single peek for half an hour."

Invariably he would drop off to sleep for the most of two hours. The children still laugh about this one, for anyone knows that the inevitable result for a normal child is to go to sleep. We have an idea they will use this device on their children.

We have cared for children who did not have good nap habits, and have been forced to use other methods. One child settled down when Dorothy would lie down with her, put her hand on her back, and say, "Let's cuddle like spoons." If necessary, Dorothy would get up as soon as the child fell asleep, but she often enjoyed a little rest herself. Sometimes she found a little singing or reading would make a child relax enough to submit to his natural fatigue, and provide an effective prelude to a nap.

Our daughter Kathleen (her married name is Kordenbrock) was until recently (when she had her first child) an early childhood specialist with the Sacramento City Schools in a minority area that was considered by some educators to be "difficult." Knowing the importance of rest, particularly for kindergarteners that tended to be hyperactive, she set out to insure that everyone had a daily nap. Some of the parents said their children would never sleep. But a very simple routine soon had all soundly at rest.

First, she promised a story as soon as everyone was quiet on his pad and covered by some personal item—usually a blanket, towel or other covering from home. And with the help of her assistant she promised a back rub to every child who kept his eyes closed and was absolutely quiet. Even a little wiggling was not allowed. The youngsters enjoyed the personal touch of teachers' hands, and shortly all were sound asleep. Part of the agreement called for silence when they awoke—only whispers and quiet play—another excellent exercise in self-control. Thus the sleep of others was not interrupted. She saw some sleep on for over two hours!

We have frequently used little animal stories like this to help lull a sleepless child. Tell it very slowly and as softly as duck's down: "Out on the farm there were two little white woolly lambs. They were so cute and soft. They nibbled the lovely green grass in the field. They jumped and romped and played. Then they jumped and romped and played some more. Then some more . . . and some more . . . and some more. . . . Pretty soon they became very, v e r y   t i r e d, so they went to their mother and lay very close to her. Then their eyelids became very heavy and soon they closed their eyes. And before long they went to sleep. Sh, sh, sh [whisper slowly]—little white lambs are fast asleep beside the woolly mother sheep. Can you pretend you're one of those little white lambs so cozy and sleepy?" The same idea can be adapted to a puppy, kitty, or other familiar animal.

The Best Control

The first and earliest step in learning self-control—*regularity* in schedule—should be continued through life for optimum health, efficiency, and self-discipline. The second step, that of learning obedience to what the parent says, simply because he says it, should have been firmly established by age three. The child is not old enough to reason consistently, so up to this age obedience must simply become a habit. Yet, if this has not happened, you should not give up. It will be more difficult than if you had begun right, but it is not too late to make some definite changes—mostly in yourselves as parents. There should be no harshness, but patient, firm insistence on prompt obedience. This is vital not only in terms of discipline but also for safety reasons. A disobedient child is an accident going someplace to happen.

The third step—learning about rules—gradually displaces just-because-you-say-so type of obedience. The child must not continue completely under your benevolent dictatorship or he will not learn to control himself. When he is about three and a half or four you should explain the reason for rules and why obedience is necessary. He may not understand completely for some time, and it *does* take more time to explain, but this is an important step on the road to self-government. Learning the value of rules is something many children never really come to appreciate. Such an attitude toward self-control has brought a great deal of lawlessness.

Your youngster has already learned some cause and effect relationships. He knows that if you drop a glass, it will break; if you spill the milk, it must be wiped up; if you drop your food on the ground, it must be washed or thrown away. Insofar as it is safe, you should help him to learn that acts have consequences by allowing him to accept the responsibility for his acts. Sometimes this hurts parents more than the child. For instance, he is all ready to go to church. You tell him he must not walk in the wet grass or the puddles with his best shoes on. You tell him why. But he disobeys and the shoes get all wet. He can't go with wet shoes for he might catch cold. So he must wear his old shoes, which embarrass you. So be it. Let him polish them as best he can and use the old shoes. On occasion he may not be able to go at all—which could mean that you also may have to remain away from a cherished event. That is sometimes the price of effective parenting. But this strategy is ever so much better than scolding or spanking, for it does not involve something you are doing to him bodily. He sees that he has brought on the unpleasant results.

Spanking has its legitimate place, but it is often overdone and sometimes underdone. It should not substitute for proper training, nor should you use it to vent your frustration over childhood error and limitations.

Generally speaking, a spanking should be administered as a last resort—not as a habit. If a child clearly understands what is expected of him and deliberately and defiantly disobeys, this may be the appropriate time for spanking. Even then, if you reason with him firmly and kindly and he is able to see his fault, he may not need corporal punishment. But be careful not to threaten spanking unless you are ready to follow through.

A small switch that stings when applied to bare legs or bottom but does not injure is the proper "weapon." Your adult hand is usually much too strong. Completely ruling out spanking helps you avoid impulsive, frequent, or random slaps or hits for relatively minor infractions. You must be in control of yourself before you can teach self-control to your child. Though physical pain is necessarily involved, it should be appropriate for the size of the child. A little goes a long way when also accompanied by temporary loss of valued approval. But remember, you are not rejecting the child—only his behavior. So always end the ordeal by hugging your child and assuring him of your love and forgiveness as well as encouraging him to obey the next time.

In this connection, help the child to see that everything need not be learned the hard way. Discuss real life experiences you, your family, and friends may have had that will teach lessons of safety, thrift, honesty, dependability, and other character qualities. Dennis and Kathie were deeply impressed with the story of how I was run over by a car because I had disobeyed my father's orders not to ride a bicycle on the street. Include stories from inspiring books such as the Bible and tell them while you are working or playing together, for example, on the obedience of Moses, the courage of young David, the honesty of Daniel, the humility of John the Baptist.

Little Speech-Maker

Speech is a skill that takes time as well as training to develop properly. School success, social relationships and your child's own sense of self-worth depend greatly on his language ability. No matter what you, the parent, may do, you can't hurry speech beyond a certain point. But once the mechanical apparatus and the association areas of the brain are ready to function, what you do makes a great deal of difference in the *quality* of the speech and the rate of development. Appropriate stimulation and encouragement are, as we have suggested, needed from birth.

Some children are delayed in speech because they are left alone too much and are not talked to. Others find they can get what they want without bothering to ask for it, and thus have no reason to speak. Still others are allowed to talk baby talk and even hear it repeated to them, so they have no incentive to improve.

First of all, parents have the responsibility to guide the child's speech by their example. If your speech is fast, slurred or indistinct, too soft or too loud, your child will not even hear the words correctly, and his imitation will be comparatively poor. You will need to speak slowly, clearly, and precisely. Almost anyone can afford to improve his speech either by special awareness and self-discipline or by local night school classes for adults. It is easier to start your child right than for him to require speech therapy later on.

Second, you will need to help him speak correctly. As much as possible you should do this indirectly so as not to make him feel self-conscious or put down. For instance, repeat your youngster's remarks in correct form. If he says, "Sally don't like cookies," say, "Sally *doesn't* like cookies? I wonder why." Or if he says, "Our puppies is hungry," answer, "Oh, our puppies *are* hungry, *are* they?" In some cases there is nothing else to do but to tactfully suggest a better way. Parents also need to discourage egocentric or socially unacceptable speech, such as bragging, name-calling, exaggeration or vulgarisms. Be so careful about who provides his models. Few schools with their large numbers of children per teacher can desirably substitute for your all-round example.

Also use exact words for color, size, shape, or objects: "I'll give you some zucchini," instead of "I'll give you some of this." Or, "Please put this road atlas on Daddy's desk," instead of "Please put this thing on Daddy's desk." In any case, remember that articulation, the ability to hear and make all the speech sounds, is generally not complete until about age eight. The implication of this for formal schooling is the same as for other abilities. It is difficult to learn to read when any necessary tool is yet untempered or not fully developed.

Toy telephones, even a pair of hot drink cups connected by a string, encourage conversation between family members or playmates. Learning to answer the real telephone by identifying himself, then the other speaker, and passing the phone to the proper person is good practice for your young secretary. If there are relatives or friends nearby, reporting daily activities to them will be an incentive in developing language skills, practicing common courtesies, and in learning more about your extended family. Don't let the television set usurp your very important conversations during these all-important years for gaining skill in listening and speaking.

Learning fingerplays and verses is good practice for speech as well as for strengthening the memory and for training the ear to hear rhyming words and rhythm. To help your child memorize a verse, say the whole thing through to him first to give the full meaning. Then say one line at a time and have him repeat it after you, echo style. Repeat the whole verse in the same way once or twice more, but not enough to tire him. Repeat the same process the next day or later in the day if he asks for it. After two or three days he will be able to say it *with* you. Such memorization is painless, and the process develops your child's skill in being able to repeat several words after you. Here are some little rhymes which emphasize speech sounds. Other verses and songs can be found in many children's books:

> A farmer went trotting,
> Upon his grey mare,
> Bumpety, bumpety, bump!
> With his daughter behind him
> So rosey and fair,
> Bumpety, bumpety, bump!
>
> As I was going along, along
> A-singing a comical song, song, song.

The lane that I went was so long, long, long.
And the song that I sang was so long, long, long
And so I went singing along.

The great tall clock in the hall
The grandfather's clock of them all
Goes tick-tock, tick-tock [*slowly and in deep voice*]
But mother's little clock on the shelf
Goes tick-tock, tick-tick-tock [*faster, medium voice*]
And father's little watch in his pocket
Goes ticky, ticky, ticky, tocket [*very fast, high voice*].

A humming top am I
My voice is sweet and low—m-m-m-m.
                                   (All anonymous)

A Positive Social Creature

Many conscientious parents have been convinced that nursery school is a must for their three-year-old. Some make financial deposits and apply well ahead of time to be sure their little jewels are admitted early to institutional life. They have been persuaded by the ongoing myth that children of that age must be exposed to many other little ones in order to be socialized. The truth is that these children are indeed socialized, but not in the way most parents would wish. We reemphasize here in different form some crucial needs and methods we have mentioned earlier. Let's see again how socialization works.

The ability to form healthy interpersonal relationships is initially based on mother-infant bonding—that close, unique relationship which influences both mother and child a great deal more than was thought possible not too many years ago. Gentle, loving, consistent, and responsive care through early childhood, by both mother and father, nurtures and promotes this emotional attachment. The security, self-respect, and sense of self-worth gained from this kind of home life until children stabilize their values and are able to reason consistently lays the groundwork for positive socialization.

The young child learns by observation and imitation. He learns all the time, whether we plan to teach him or not. When he is put with a group of little children he imitates *them*. He has no way of sorting out the bad from the good. As a matter of fact, we know that he learns the bad more easily than the good. And in general little children are clearly not models of good social and moral values. They are naturally self-centered. They have not yet developed much of a conscience. They adapt quickly to bad habits, manners, language, and morals. They don't know the meaning of rules or even the Golden Rule. Nor do they understand cooperation.

So even a few hours a week in nursery school dilutes your child's attachment to you and causes him to latch onto the values of his peers. Because he is not able to reason, he does not understand your remonstrance or explanation of his actions. In fact, he is more confused than helped and may simply be upset at you. After all, he reasons immaturely, it must be all right because "all the other kids are doing it." Then your values get the back of his little hand. Such early dependence on peers has become more and more common as the tendency to earlier schooling has increased. In some extreme cases of too much out-of-home group care, older children cannot make decisions or think independently. Peer dependency is a social cancer and harder to remedy than the dread disease. There is perhaps no greater limit of human potential.

Association with anyone other than a child's family is not normally required. He needs good adult models to imitate— preferably his parents. Like any little animal or bird, his tender nerves and emotions thrive best in a simple, quiet environment. He cannot at this age relate well to even relatively small groups of children without strain. It often makes him overexcited; sometimes nervous, fearful, or apprehensive.

We do not suggest putting your child in a social strait jacket. A reasonable amount of association with other children of neighbors, relatives, and friends is healthy—especially so when your child has no brothers and sisters. This provides a "mirror" in which he can see himself and helps him learn to relate to different kinds of people. But because he is so impressionable, you should be selective about his associates. Many parents have learned sadly and too late how children acquire bad language or habits, rude manners, and deceitfulness. Your child is not likely to be an exception without your watchful care. His play should be carefully supervised by you, not necessarily directing or interfering, but within sight and sound. The time involved and the number of children should be limited. Generally, your child will play better with only one other child. A rough rule-of-thumb for the maximum number, even at a birthday party, for example, is the same number of children as your child's age, that is, three for a three-year-old, four for a four-year-old, and so on.

In addition to the fact that children do not learn positive socialization by being exposed to large groups of children such as in a nursery school, there is strong evidence that they lose initiative and creativity. And even worse, the chances that the child will interpret his being sent to nursery school as rejection by his parents is very great. Martin Engel, head of the National Day Care Demonstration Center, strongly states that this is true no matter how much we rationalize otherwise. Many children become emotionally upset in various ways by such separation from their parents. Care-givers witness these mini-tragedies every day but few seem to really understand. Listen to this letter we received from a former teacher-aide in California. Bear in mind that a University Center is set up as a demonstration for University students to observe, practice, and copy. This one was related to a major medical school and was widely acclaimed among professionals and in the press as a model. Its director had a doctor's degree in early childhood education. Our correspondent was a college graduate teacher. She wrote:

I worked as a Teacher-aide in the University Day Care Center . . . for 9 months after we were married. I'm so glad I got that experience. It taught me that even the BEST day care center (which this was supposed to be) cannot begin to compare with a good home and mother. I would never subject my child to the rigid schedules, competition, regimentation and discipline of any day care center. I saw the sad effects it had on even the most well-adjusted, good children. I enjoyed my work there and I gave so much of myself to those children. I grew to love them dearly, but how sad it was to see tired mothers who'd worked all day, pick up their children at night and not have much energy or interest to give their children. Anxious little ones showed their paintings and drawings to mom who smiled and said, "That's nice dear," and hurried them off to McDonald's for supper. It used to tear my heart out. I also saw the effects of divorce on a child. Father was a medical student and mother worked. Their separation and divorce was written all over their daughter in her regressive behavior and mental agony.

I once heard this statement. "Children are the most abused and discriminated-against minority of all minority groups." I think it's true, only children don't have the ability to make their plight known as do other minority groups.

We recognize that circumstances in many homes make it impossible for the child to stay home all day. Generally, the next best care can be provided in another warm, responsive home. If this is not available, find a school or day care center where the circumstances are as nearly like the home as possible. There should be the same teachers day after day—not a variety of teacher aides or part-time parents. When a favored teacher is absent, the little child experiences serious attachment loss. When this experience is repeated often and over a long enough period of time, many youngsters learn to become attached to no one any more. For them love and trust are lost arts. Such were many children after World War II who flowered into the rebels of the sixties. And many children of today who turn to alcohol and drugs. Making and breaking attachments is far more damaging to the child's emotional stability than most parents and teachers understand.

In an ideal situation, the teacher should have motherly qualities and not more than five or six children, preferably of varying ages, to care for. The little nucleus should be somewhat separated from the large school group as in a separate room of a house. In one experimental program we observed in Melbourne, Australia, the city was renting houses near the children's homes instead of building schools for care centers. The different rooms readily adapted to smaller groups and a more familylike atmosphere. As much as possible the ideal program and activities should resemble a good mother's home program—involvement in homemaking activities, including gardening and other useful work; nature experiences; rest; and freedom from academic pressures.

Dealing with Fear

There are some children who seem to feel less secure than others regardless of how they have been treated. Force in this case is no more effective than it is in any other part of child training. And as with other problems, fearfulness is easier to prevent than cure.

We have already presented principles we believe to be essential to a warm, loving parent-child relationship. The more secure and stable this attachment is, the less the fears of anything will develop. Your attitude, of course, is vital, and it is better caught than formally taught. If you are fearful of thunder, or of certain animals or things, your child will imitate. An overanxious parent who is constantly warning the child (or others) about being careful and of the possibility of getting hurt can cause the child to be apprehensive even if he doesn't know what it is he fears. Perhaps a certain reasonableness about what is important to be afraid of and what is not should first be faced by you. Valid precautions are sensible for anyone to take, but undue fearfulness takes much of the joy out of life. Those who, without presumption, put their trust in God's protection find a special peace and contentment.

There are several causes of fear. Some seem to appear no matter what you do or don't do. For instance, the infant seems to be born with the fear of falling. Also, loud noise, the presence of a stranger, or the sound of a machine may startle him. Other fears definitely can be avoided. Premature exposure to what some older children and adults consider exciting experiences may be traumatic to a baby or young child. Fireworks, the circus, the merry-go-round, the zoo, or anywhere there is too much noise, too many people or too much confusion, and many television programs—even children's TV—are more fearful than fun. The trouble is that unless we take precautions about these things, they will multiply, spreading like an infection in the child's life. So a simple, quiet, uncluttered home environment, reducing as much as possible the causes of fear is obviously the answer for the development of a stable, confident child.

One of the reasons for fear is the child's lack of knowledge and his inability to understand or reason. He does not know what causes the loud noise of thunder or the characteristics of certain animals or things that are new or strange. Fear of the dark, for example, is largely fear of the unknown. The dark can be made to appear beautiful if the child can become acquainted with it while his curiosity is high and his inhibitions few. In the security of daddy's arms he will enjoy a pre-bedtime outdoor walk when dark comes early enough. Help him identify the croaking of frogs and the chirp of the crickets. Listen for other sounds of the night. You might take along a flashlight to locate some of the singing insects. Perhaps you live in an area where fireflies do their fascinating dances on the grass and through the trees. Spectacular sights of the moon shining through the trees or over the water and the starry heavens all combine to make the dark a natural and exciting experience to the child.

One evening an unusually bold thunderstorm descended upon our Michigan home. The thunder sounded like a caravan of ten-wheel trucks roaring over our roof. A four-year-old visiting us from California was at first alarmed. We knew that it is normal for small youngsters to have fears and that it is usually better to distract or divert them than to meet their apprehensions head-on. So Dorothy called the little girl over to her.

"Heidi," she asked, "would you like to play sort of a game with God?"

"Yes," she answered, partly in wonder and partly in anticipation.

"Then turn out the lights over there." Dorothy was involving

Heidi in the action instead of herself turning the lights out on the little child.

Heidi expectantly obeyed.

"Now sit down here by me." Dorothy invited the little girl into her swivel rocker that she turned to the front windows overlooking our lake. Cuddled in Dorothy's arms, and already involved in the actions, Heidi had largely forgotten her fears and was ready to learn about the dazzling display of lightning which reflected from the heavens to the water and made the yard almost as clear as day.

"See," Dorothy nodded toward the storm. "God is making a great big spark of electricity." She went on to explain what she meant by a "spark," and Heidi readily grasped the similarity to things she'd already experienced. Most three or four-year-olds can make the connection between the little sparks we sometimes make when we take off a synthetic sweater in the dark on a dry winter night and the display in the sky. They will also be intrigued at such times if you shuffle across the rug and touch each other, creating a spark between your fingers and theirs—or kissing, to find that there can be more than emotional shock to a kiss.

Later we explain that lightning heats and moves the air so suddenly that it makes the thunder noise. We sometimes blow up a couple of paper bags and pop them to help the child understand. An older child can also learn that a person caught in a lightning storm should not take shelter under a tree because lightning finds ways to travel to the ground, usually through a tall object. We teach that a car is one of the safest places because lightning cannot easily travel through the tires to the ground. In one family we know, the youngest child was afraid of thunder until, during a storm, an older brother suggested that they all clap their hands to see if they could make more noise than the thunder. They tried and laughed. How could thunder be very bad if clapping can make so much noise too?

Children who regularly watch television have been found to be more fearful of what might happen to them than those who rarely see it. Untrue, frightening stories (including classics such as Red Riding Hood) or gruesome pictures may also cause an exaggerated sense of danger. And things that might not seem fearful to an adult are frightening for a child because he cannot anticipate the "happy ending." We have seen several instances where well-adjusted children responded with fear to something relatively mild from an adult's point of view. One terrified child ran from the room in tears when a truck rolled down the hill in a Disney film.

In case certain fears have already developed, the child needs sympathetic, patient understanding. He should never be teased or chided. And since he is not a consistently reasoning creature until about age eight or nine, a rational explanation may be useless. But you might tell him about someone (perhaps yourself) with a similar fear who conquered it in time. Keep the example short, and assure the child of your support, but without making too much of it. If he fears an animal or object that is harmless, talk assuringly and show him how you can touch it without harm. You may encourage him to approach it, but never bring it closer to him. He must work up the courage himself, perhaps over a period of time.

Almost anyone can have a bad dream occasionally. Often the cause in children is a reaction to daytime fears, an insecure or damaged relationship with you, some disturbing experience or excess fatigue from too little rest or too much stimulation. The problem with young children under seven or eight is that their reasoning powers have not developed sufficiently to understand the explanations we could give. At this age also, they cannot easily distinguish between reality and dreams.

We recommend that you go to your child immediately, for the panic in his cry will identify a valid problem. Pat him, talk to him, comfort him, assure him and, if necessary, stay with him until he falls asleep. But be careful about reinforcing any behavior which you would rather not have continued. It is wise to soothe him with the least attention possible, for if you rock him, walk the floor with him, take him into bed with you, or give him food, you may find yourself doing it for many months to come. If bad dreams come frequently, give special attention to removing the cause. Carefully monitor daytime activities, health habits, influence of companions, family relationships, and methods of discipline.

How Work Builds

Children play naturally and experts often remind us that their play is serious business. They imitate grown-ups: in essence it is their work. So if you don't spoil their enthusiasm by instilling negative attitudes, there will be no basic difference to them in work and play. Both will be pleasurable activities.

It is true that we generally think of work as being more practical, necessary, and productive. Some people are fortunate enough to be able to make their living with work they truly enjoy and some love to work at most anything. Since labor occupies most of us nearly one-third of our lives, a good work attitude contributes to our happiness. To instill the joy of working early in life is a very special accomplishment.

Work experience provides a young child advantages in his learning as well as in helping him find enjoyment in working. Work enriches his thinking powers, enhances his moral values, increases his self-direction, and makes him more efficient in planning and problem-solving. Even more important, it is a prime factor in character development. An idle mind is still the devil's workshop. The constructively busy child is the child who is better behaved.

There may be small jobs he can do alone by now, but in general you (this can be either parent) should work with him. You and he can make your bed together, sweep the porch or fix the meal together. You can wash the car, work the garden, or make things with him. Compliment his work (not him personally) and thank him. His greatest reward is the feeling of having done something that is worthwhile and appreciated. This is the kind of success which encourages and highly motivates.

There seems to be an opportune time for children to learn certain skills. Such readiness is not always easy to detect, but alert, conscientious parents who are in close contact with their child daily will generally have little trouble. On the other hand, even the most skilled teacher cannot possibly keep such close track of a large number of children.

For example, your child can learn to tie his shoes when he is about four years old and normally not later than five. If teaching him is too frustrating for you, get a bright six- or seven-year-old to teach him. Parents who continue to tie his shoes for him are doing him a disservice by crippling his self-reliance and independence. Whatever he is capable of doing as part of the home team in self-help or family help, he should be trained to do.

Following Directions

One of the most delightful jobs for the young child is doing errands, especially if he knows what he is doing is really helpful and appreciated. Start with simple, one-step directions and be sure you have your youngster's attention before telling him what to do. One mother we know invariably asks the child to look at her before she gives him any kind of instruction. Then she speaks slowly and clearly. This helps to eliminate repeating the request—a bad habit to establish. The ability to listen and follow directions with only one request is valuable training which can start early in life.

As your little one develops skill, give him two-step directions and later still more complicated instructions: "Please bring my red book from the night stand by my bed." Or, "Please put this box on the washing machine in the back porch." Later on you can add still another step: "And also bring me the jacket from the dryer." Don't add the extra step until you are quite sure he can handle it. It takes careful listening to follow such requests, but the training will bring you rich rewards and make parenting more satisfying than frustrating, and much more fun. In the process of teaching your child to follow directions, you will need to help him understand front and back, up and down, under and over, right side up and upside down, and, eventually, right and left. Let him learn to give directions also—how to get to the post office, the church, or other places with which he is acquainted.

When the errands involve numbers, you are teaching mathematical concepts. The basic understanding of numbers is fundamental to formal arithmetic. Many children have trouble in school because they have not had enough real experiences with numbers to understand, for example, the "fourness" of four. So use such requests and activities often. "Please bring me four big potatoes from the vegetable bin—one for each member of the family." Incidentally, why not let him scrub them for baking or peel them with a regular peeler—which is safer than a knife. In general, do this sort of thing when your child is participating with you in your work—which should be many of his waking moments. However, do not break his concentration if he is absorbed in an appropriate activity. This distracts him and could cause him to form the habit of being easily distracted, and hyperactive—jumping from one thing to another.

Learning to Share

Selfishness probably causes more trouble in this world than any other one characteristic. Narcissism—the "me-first" syndrome—is the bane of our society. The test of each individual's maturity is the extent to which he has progressed away from this negative trait toward the highest rung of character development—that of unselfish concern and service for others. Though only a relatively small number of people reach this state, it is the ideal for which we should aim.

Children are born totally self-centered. They have no conscience and they use others for self-gratification. But they do not know when they are making selfish demands—even depriving parents of their rights in order to indulge them. It is up to the parents to determine which desires are legitimate or which, if fulfilled, will simply encourage the child's egocentric nature. Then parents need to help them continue to develop normally in character qualities. To do this effectively, they should know about children's capacity and readiness to achieve these desirable traits.

The love and trust that is established by the consistent, loving care of his parents is basic to the child's sense of values. Then in the first three years he can learn, at least partially, to delay his wants, to respect others' property, and willingly to relinquish an item his parent or other care-giver asks for. These are important steps and should not be neglected. The child's natural sensitivity helps him learn quickly what is expected of him. However, it is relatively futile to expect a child under three years old to do much sharing. He has little or no comprehension of this concept and little capacity to play cooperatively. He may actually offer a bite or piece of what he has or even a toy if requested, but his motive would be a desire to please or simply to obey rather than because he understands sharing.

When he is about three he can learn to take turns and to share. He must be helped to see the fairness of this behavior, and the pleasure that cooperating can bring. That's why he needs a lot of practice in working and playing with those who can demonstrate its value. The most effective demonstrators are his parents. The practice should be performed with brothers and sisters and/or a limited number of playmates—preferably one or two at a time, and all with parental supervision.

You might plan with your child to have a special little collection of things for him to give away. These could be little plastic toys and balloons of the kind which come in cereal boxes or even little things he has received which he could share with others. He might give one to a little visitor when he leaves, to a sick child, or to a child who does not have as many things as he does. At Christmas time, do not emphasize gifts for him, but let him help to select, wrap and give gifts to others. Even for his birthday, make it a time to thank his relatives and friends for their love and kindness to him for the year instead of centering too much attention on him. If you have a party, remember to keep it simple, short, and small—no more than four children for a four-year-old, for example.

In the process of teaching how to share, it is wise to prepare your child ahead of time. If another child, preferably one who has learned to share, is coming to play, talk about what toys he will let his friend play with. Don't suggest his favorite truck at first, but help him to set aside certain attractive items for his guest. Jog his memory a couple of times so that he will not forget and balk when the time comes. Or better yet, play-act the situation, with you as the visitor. Keep the playtime with the other child short at first. Then as he sees the fun of cooperative play, sharing will become easier and he can play longer.

Story Time

Stories are food to your youngster's mind. You don't need to be a professional to tell stories to your child. Just relate the events simply as you would tell your neighbor. Don't attempt to memorize the words. Just keep the events in order. It is best to have only one definite aim and eliminate anything that does not support this aim. A good way to begin is to read simple Bible stories or nature stories out of true story books. Then retell the stories as you put your child to bed. Young children thrive on repetition. A list of books for you and another list for children is suggested in Appendix 2. Also tell your children stories right out of your life—as no one else can tell them. They do not need contrived fantasies nor cruel or scary tales. Tell them about grandpa's sheepdog or the bricklayer working on the new house down the street or what it takes to bring a carton of milk to the table or how squirrels prepare for winter. If you are short on resources, any competent librarian will help you find what you want.

You can tell stories while your hands are occupied with almost any household task. There is no teaching method more powerful than example itself. Almost any lesson you wish to teach can be incorporated into a story. It gets across much better than direct instruction. These lessons can be on such subjects as health, safety, kindness to animals, thankfulness, and many others. They can be incidents which happened to you, your family, or friends. Or retell things which happened to him when he was younger. You don't need a large variety because children like the same ones over and over again.

Story time is also important for learning to read. The Michigan Education Association hands out a bumper sticker that is delightful and true: KIDS WHO READ WERE READ TO. Read to your child beginning when he is a baby. The experience will bring you closer to him and him to you and will condition both of you to the fun of reading together. Then as he grows, have your physician test his vision and hearing, and have plenty of good books appropriate to his age around the house. If you do this, you will almost certainly have a good reader.

This method of teaching is of special value because the child really hears what you say. He can easily follow your line of thought and it is interesting to him. He remembers the lesson because he remembers the story. Since he desires to imitate, he is likely to do as the story suggests. Of course, you must be sure your story teaches a positive lesson and that the point you wish to emphasize gets across. This is the problem with some of the highly rated television shows such as Disney or the "Muppets"—even some of the popular educational programs such as "Captain Kangaroo" or "Sesame Street." Some of the silly acting and false characters involved in the teaching of a fact are likely to be imitated, but the fact may be forgotten because the two were not logically connected. If you insist on using TV as a baby-sitter, keep it brief, and more realistic, like "Mr. Rogers." Better none at all.

The scriptural standard of Philippians 4:8 is particularly fitting, but difficult for some because it questions myths, fairy tales, and violent, weird or gruesome stories. "Whatsoever things are honest, whatsoever things are just, whatsoever things are pure, whatsoever things are lovely, whatsoever things are of good report; if there be any virtue, and if there be any praise, think on these things." Sound advice in judging the quality of the mental nourishment supplied to your child's mind. That nourishment determines the quality of the mind's health and strength.

When you read stories to your child, the same standards apply. Hold him closely while you read slowly, with good lip movement and with expression. Take time to look at the pictures, to answer and ask questions, and possibly to have a short discussion, imagining why the characters did what they did.

And in preparation for your child's later reading instruction, help him direct his eye movement from left to right when looking at books or signs. The human brain or the eyes are not programmed to make us naturally read from left to right. Japanese people, for example, read columns from top to bottom and from right to left. Training is necessary for proper progression in any language. So keep this in mind when you look at a series of pictures, or count objects with a child. Show him where to start and help him move to the right by moving his or your finger in that direction. If he scribbles in pretending to write, help him use left-to-right progression. If he asks about his name or a word, glide your finger under the word in a left-to-right motion. Otherwise, when he starts to read he will have trouble with *saw* and *was*, *not* and *ton*, etc.

Independent Thinking

We were anxious to have our children become independent thinkers in a constructive way. But we found very early that they could be selfish, too. They did not realize that they were often thinking only of themselves. At two or three or four they simply preferred to play alone with a toy even though they liked to be around other kids. They showed this self-centeredness also in their conversation. They needed to learn how to share because it is right, not only because we told them to. They needed to learn how to stop what they were doing and listen, rather than to ignore our suggestions and keep right on doing their own things—a characteristic often seen in adults who never really learned thoughtful manners, and particularly in senile oldsters who are returning to childish ways.

We decided to put our children to work—with us in the home—and to find opportunities for them to help or serve others. When together you and your children share duties and service, such as in the kitchen or the garage or the community, they blossom. They develop a sense of self-worth; they feel identified with you and the family corporation. They feel needed, wanted, and depended on. Ego concern is quieted and thoughtfulness thrives. These children are the ones who become the powerful social leaders.

The young child understands only one meaning for a word and

does not comprehend symbolism at all. This is why he cannot always accept adult teasing or jokes, even though he may think that his own jokes or actions are hilarious. He is very gullible, accepting almost everything that he sees and hears. He is likely to believe television commercials completely. Then when he finds out after much exposure to such things that they are not all true, he is tempted not to trust anyone or anything, because he is not capable of sorting out the false from the true.

An especially interesting characteristic of the young child's thinking is his assumption that certain separated objects are one and the same. For example, before his plane took off on a trip from Chicago's O'Hare Airport to Los Angeles International, a four-year-old boy noticed the red and yellow semitrailer gasoline truck which was refueling one of the nearby planes. When his plane arrived in Los Angeles, the boy looked out of the window and immediately noticed a red and yellow semitrailer gasoline truck. He excitedly remarked, "Wow! Look how fast that gas truck is! It got here before we did." If you and the child go for a walk in the woods and see a rabbit, then a little later see another, and still later another, he will very probably conclude that the same rabbit was following him all the way.

Your three- or four-year-old cannot understand comparisons or logical or abstract thinking. He cannot discuss a subject that requires consistent logic or reasoning or see another's viewpoint until he approaches age seven or eight or more. He has a one-track mind and is not usually capable of taking in more than one aspect of a situation at one time.

Since we want to help and encourage him to develop his reasoning ability, we must give him as many real-life experiences as possible that build his background of knowledge. Don't supply immediate answers to all of his questions. But do not ignore them, even if they are a means of getting needed attention. Instead, some of the time try turning the questions back to him. Or suggest how he might find the answer. Or sometimes just ask him questions— especially "why" and "how" questions, for example, "Why isn't grass pink?"

Sometimes the questions should be a starting point for experimentation or exploration. To discover some of the answers by this method may take longer, and your child may seem to be wasting time, but don't despair. Ready-made knowledge does not usually stimulate thinking. Sometimes the trial-and-error method will be a good way for him to learn. If he is learning to set the table or wash dishes, certain risks are involved. You should be close at hand to provide guidance, perhaps with more questions or suggestions, but restrain yourself from providing all the solutions. The process of independently working out problems will strengthen his mental powers.

All adults sometimes need solitude, but often they do not realize that a child has a similar or even more critical requirement for time alone—time for the kind of somewhat undirected, imaginative thinking that helps him adapt to real-life experiences. Or it may simply provide relief from stimulation. An excellent laboratory for this is a sand pile with its potential for tunnels and roads, or the kitchen sink where he fills and empties containers near you, or on the floor with blocks of wood or toys. This seems to provide the opportunity he needs to work out certain problems and fantasies, though he would be incapable of explaining this process to anyone else. Confronted with a problem situation, he employs this kind of soliloquy to sort out and organize the information he has received. It is a problem-solving device and a way of establishing attitudes. This essential privilege is rarely offered in a day-care center, nursery school, or in any large group of children.

Those Play Things

Your three-year-old is ready to make good use of play equipment that is designed to use his large muscles vigorously. Don't deprive him of climbing—just help him to do it safely and within limits. Country living usually provides small trees and fences for this activity, but city parks or playgrounds with a jungle gym, slide, swing, or teeter-totter will also do the trick.

Housekeeping toys and things for playing store are easily

available if you can encourage the use of the imagination. Cardboard boxes can be used to represent anything from the kitchen sink or stove to the sofa. Empty cans can fill "store" shelves. Discarded adult clothes for dressing up appeal to this age child. He can impersonate adults in various occupations with one or two typical items such as a homemade paper fire hat and a short piece of garden hose to pretend being a fireman.

Woodworking tools become appropriate now. You may prefer to have your child use a wooden hammer and pegs with a pegboard at first. Later he can proceed to using a steel hammer with a short handle and broad head and short, wide-headed nails. Just pounding nails into soft wood is valuable practice in coordination. Soon a pointed piece of 1" × 4" board, a foot or so long, with a small block and a spool on top, will be to him a marvelous new boat to float in the bathtub or play pool. A simple airplane, wagon, or truck can be constructed of small pieces of scrap wood and spools. With daddy's help he can make a bird feeder. Not only will the child be providing a fascinating experience in bird-watching for the whole family, but he can begin to take the responsibility of keeping the feeder filled with bird seed.

Any household can provide an assortment of various-sized plastic containers with screw-on lids. Put them all in a box unassembled and let your child match the right lid to the right jar. Nuts and bolts of various sizes can be matched in the same way. Later on have him try it blindfolded.

A pair of daddy's old, clean shoes with plenty of lacing will give practice in muscle coordination as well as in learning to tie a bow toward the end of this period. Magazines with colored pictures and blunt scissors to cut them out and paste on a piece of paper, in a scrapbook, or to make a collage are good for a rainy day.

A child this age can draw or paint pictures with large crayons or washable poster paints and large brushes. Give him large sheets of wrapping paper, the blank side of wallpaper remnants, or unfolded grocery sacks to use on the floor or on an easel made of cardboard or plywood. He needs freedom of arm movement, which small equipment does not provide. Brushes can be made by tying or taping strips of cloth or pieces of sponge to a stick. Start with one or two colors, with a separate brush for each one.

Recently we listened in on a typical preschool conversation. A visitor was trying to make conversation with a budding sculptor who had his four-year-old hands deep in clay.

"What are you making?" the guest inquired.

"Don't you know?" came the counter-question.

"Well—"

"Aw, can't you see?"

At that point the visitor realized that she was in fact an intruder and would have been wiser to place her emphasis on the process rather than the product. Even the teacher didn't know that it was a flying saucer. But she did quickly ask some good questions.

"Tell me, Bixby, what else are we going to need to finish your thing? More clay? Other colors?"

When her indirect questioning did not bring out the identity of his project, the teacher turned to several nearby youngsters and suggested "a guessing game." "Who," she wondered out loud, "can imagine what Bix is making?" Succumbing to this indirect approach, the young sculptor quickly joined in the fun and soon revealed his project's identity. In fact, another four-year-old was the one who guessed correctly.

Whether the medium is stringing beads, making a picture, or arranging sticks, remember that it is the process in such creative work rather than the end result that is most important to the preschooler. You can't even be sure about making comments about what he is doing or ask him what he is making. The answer could very well be, "How do I know? I haven't finished yet." Often a child in nursery school cannot recognize his picture the day after he has made it.

When he completes one of his creations, ask him to tell you about his picture. In this way you avoid the serious risk of offending or discouraging him by guessing wrongly. Commend the art work and display it proudly on a wall or bulletin board.

Although he is not a little adult, he is beginning to become "his own man" . . . or she, "her own woman." Study your child's developmental needs. Give nature time and as a parent "stay by the stuff." Closeness, warmth, responsiveness and consistency will pay enormous dividends in the years just ahead as your little one becomes a bigger one and moves on to adulthood.

Challenging the Senses

Since all learning comes by way of the senses you will need to be aware of ways to stimulate but not unduly pressure these valuable avenues to the brain. Probably the most attractive and all-inclusive medium for such training is the natural world around us. The colors, sounds, textures, smells, and tastes found in God's creation should consume the larger share of your time and attention. Collecting the "treasures" found in outdoor walks or excursions is so normal that you will certainly allow and encourage this and the curiosity that goes with it. You can help your child press his wild flowers and leaves and provide a place to keep them. Later he can identify, classify, and arrange his rocks, shells, or whatever he cherishes in a display.

But for rainy days and when you are looking for something different to do, you and your child can still find ways to challenge his senses. Puzzles and games made with household materials are fun and easy to make. For example, take a large cardboard and let him trace with a felt pen or crayon various-sized shapes of different objects you have around the house—simple cookie cutters, lids, small boxes. Provide something triangular as well as round or rectangular. Kitchen sponges can be cut up for this. Do only a few at first to make it easy to succeed. Add more shapes as ability increases. Keep the objects in a special box and match the shapes to the pattern drawn on the cardboard. Both size and shape must be considered. Later he will learn the names of the shapes—square, oblong, circle, triangle and oval.

Jigsaw puzzles can be made of large, uncluttered magazine pictures pasted smoothly on cardboard and cut into smaller parts. Depending on his former experiences, he may be able to piece together ten pieces or more. But start where he can succeed rather quickly and later cut the puzzle into more pieces.

At meal time occasionally have your child close his eyes or blindfold him a few minutes to have a "guess what" taste and smell game. Use distinctive foods, not mixtures, and only a few at a time, and see if he can identify each one, first by smell and then by taste. Also have him tell you whether each is sweet, sour, salty, or none of these. The only other taste we can describe is bitter and we do not usually eat bitter foods, though some clean orange peel may give the idea and be perfectly harmless. Also help him to describe food as crisp or crunchy, hard or soft, wet or dry. See if he can guess what is cooking or baking if he has not watched or helped with the preparation.

Some foods can be named by feeling—fruits, vegetables, beans, rice, oatmeal, a hard-cooked egg, or nuts, either in the shell or shelled. Acquaintance with all this practical information is valuable preparation as a background for later rapid formal learning.

To enhance the sense of touch and to increase vocabulary, children should become acquainted with textures. Cloth offers a variety—burlap, net, corduroy, satin, velvet, felt, silk, wool, and cotton. Then there are smooth leather, suede leather, plastic, sandpaper, fur, etc. Cut two squares of as many of these as possible, using pinking shears on the cloth ones if you have them. Since we often use "silky," "velvety," "woolly," etc., to describe textures, it is good for children to become acquainted with these words. But even before they can all be named, your child can match them by touch while he is blindfolded.

You might want to get from a painter or hardware store two squares each of very fine and very rough sandpaper and several grades of coarseness in between. Have the child put them in order of roughness as well as match those of the same degree of coarseness. Sometimes you can play a game of finding textures in the house. Ask the child to find something that is very smooth—or rough, soft, hard, stiff, woolly, etc.

Help your preschooler learn to hear accurately by asking him to tell you what is going on in the kitchen. He can identify corn popping, a boiling sound, even a simmering sound, the sound of frying, the toaster popping up, the refrigerator motor, perhaps a garbage disposal or dishwasher and running water. See if he can recognize the sound of a tap on glass, on metal, on plastic or wood.

Sometimes continue the question game outdoors and on trips to help the child learn to identify various noises—around the farm, at the zoo, in transportation and also in the natural world. As he grows older, he may be able to identify birds by their songs.

Built-in Safety Features

Children's immaturities in auditory and visual perception—in acutely hearing and in accurately seeing and organizing information—not only influence their ability to do school tasks but also prominently affect their safety. Until a child is at least seven or eight he has limited vision from the corners of his eyes and he takes longer than an adult to interpret what he sees. His partly insulated nerve pathways do not convey sensations so efficiently as those of an older child or adult. In other words, he may see a car coming down the street but not soon enough to do anything about it.

Also until at least age seven or eight or older he cannot localize sound easily. If he hears the sound of a car, for instance, it may not be easy for him to tell which direction it is coming from or how near it is. Add to that the fact that a child doesn't really have any concept of danger until he's at least six, and it is relatively simple to understand why vehicular traffic is the number one cause of accidents to children in the age group from one to fifteen. There is even some reason to believe that the real meaning and application of safety rules is relatively unclear until age eight or nine. For example, a nine-year-old told his father that high voltage means high off the ground where it can't hurt you. Correlating that with the fact already presented that boys mature more slowly than girls, take note that boys have more street-crossing accidents and tend to be more seriously injured than girls.

This does not mean we should hover over and worry about our children every moment. But it does mean that we should take time and effort to teach safety habits by every means possible. Example is crucial here. If there are no cars in sight, do you walk against the red light, for instance? Explain safety symbols and warnings at home, while walking, or while driving. Talk about not touching household cleaner bottles and any unfamiliar containers that are not *known* to contain good food or drink. Don't tell the child that medicine tastes good. He's really not highly discriminating about taste. That's why children will drink some pretty awful things like cleaning fluids or other poisonous substances. He might drink a whole bottle of cough medicine if you tell him it's just like candy. If you take pills, why shouldn't he? Maybe a whole bottle full. After all, they are supposed to be "candy" too.

In training for crossing the street, much practice together is needed—the child telling you what the traffic signs mean and when it is safe to cross. He should know that even when the light says "Go" or "Walk," he must still look carefully in case a driver makes a mistake. Especially warn against retrieving a ball or other toy from the street, no matter how valuable, without looking carefully first.

In case the child has a minor accident, talk it over with him and help him analyze why it happened and how it could have been avoided. Punishment even for disobedience is implicit in the bruises or cuts suffered, so you don't usually need to double up on that. Be thankful that he had a warning for the future. Whether minor or major, the causes are relatively the same, so help him learn by his experience.

Yet, don't take anything for granted. A child does not reason like an adult no matter how bright for his age you may think he is. We recently heard a story of a bright four-year-old whose mother told him he could eat a carrot right out of the garden but not with all the dirt on it. So he very carefully licked off all the dirt before eating the carrot.

Working Mothers

Last week a physician's wife called us in tears from near Riverside, California. "Dr. Moore," she began, "I'm just about to cave in. Can you listen for a few minutes?"

I allowed that I could.

"My husband is a surgeon, but we are up to our necks in bills—after medical school, internship, and residency. I could do very well specializing as a psychiatric nurse, and we could get out of debt in a couple of years. But we have two little ones, a boy nearly five and a girl three, and I have been reading your books—"

"Do you enjoy your children?" I asked. "Are you really happy with your mother role?"

"Oh, yes!"

"Do you really want to work?"

"Well . . . I do have an excellent baby-sitter available down the street, and the University preschool is considered the best."

"My question is, do you really want to work?"

"Well . . . not really."

"Do you find you are restless and want to get away from the children? Or are finances the *real* reason?"

"Mmm—" she hesitated.

"You tell me you can pay up your debts in a couple of years. Considering the potential income of a good surgeon, I wonder if this is a valid reason."

"No, really it isn't, but my friends here think I'm crazy 'rusting away in the house.' I am a pretty good nurse, and my career has already been interrupted for over five years. . . . And, Dr. Moore, I don't know if you can understand this pressure. I'm miserable."

"I think I understand a little. In fact, we find that social pressures are usually far more threatening than the law."

"Exactly . . ."

"You are going to have to make up your mind what means more to you, the welfare of your children or the biases of your neighbors, and which is the greater career, mothering or nursing."

"I know . . ."

"I hope I don't offend you."

"No, that is exactly the medicine I need. I guess I was just calling you for support."

"A mother like you is twice blessed—by God and family. So I would think at least twice before surrendering the greatest career in the world, mother—"

"Yes—motherhood—I know. Thank you again."

Similar calls or letters are a daily occurrence in our office, sometimes several times a day. And after major television or radio shows such as Donahue or Dobson they come in by the hundreds.

In addition, this mother had heard a prominent local nursery school leader say that by working outside the home and thus feeling fulfilled as a person, a mother can give her child more "quality" time and attention than if she were home all day. The inference is that this attention would be more valuable than the "quantity" care of the full-time mother. This is the sheerest of wishful thinking. There are few if any full-time jobs whose requirements are so minimal that they leave plenty of time and energy for home tasks and quality child care. People in a variety of occupations indicate that the pressure, frustrations, and time involved in their jobs leave them physically and emotionally drained. The quality of the nurture and companionship available after an eight-hour day is questionable. And the helpless child is the one who suffers most.

Of course, a child who is at home all day with a mother who is glued to the television or otherwise occupied in her own interests so that he does not receive reasonably consistent, warm responses to his needs and interests, is not receiving very much of either quantity or quality attention. Yet even in this case he knows mother is available for little confidences and comfort in case he is hurt. This provides him a certain security which is still superior to ordinary custodial day care outside of the home.

It is not really just a matter of quality versus quantity. A child needs both. Optimum nurturing is not done in concentrated doses; it is a little here and a little there. Together the parent and child interact—discovering natural wonders, asking and answering questions, sharing the household tasks, listening and telling stories, walking outdoors, having privacy but also the security of prox-imity, going to the store and participating in everyday activities during all the child's waking hours. These are learning and growing experiences that are essential to the child if he is to reach his potential. All this is especially critical in the first three years, affecting intelligence, competence, and creativity. Yet the risk of loss in these and other qualities continues until the senses are reasonably well developed and integrated and until the child is able to reason consistently. We repeat, this is generally not before ages eight to ten.

If a mother has no other choice but to work outside the home, we sympathize with her and want to give her all the help possible. Her child should have the best care society can provide. We also know that in some way she will make it up to her child the best she can—hopefully in "quality" attention rather than in material things or permissiveness. Attitude, of course, comes across loud and clear to the child. He knows whether or not his mother leaves him regretfully and how much he is really valued. No one can really deceive him about that.

After children have reached the age of eight or ten and are fully mature enough to handle the ups and downs of school life, we have no burden about what mother does when the children are away from home. If she has trained her children properly, they will carry a large share of the routine household tasks. We would wish that if she feels the need to work outside the home—either financially or emotionally—she could find something which would allow her to be at home when her children are at home. One of the most valuable moments of the child's life is when he comes in from school and calls, "Mom, I'm home." This precious opportunity for communication and understanding provides a special security to the child.

Also we would hope that the work would be of a nature that would not unduly deprive her of the energy to be a friend and counselor to her family. One of the most important functions of a wife and mother is to make home a haven for her family from the pressures of work and school. If she is also a victim of such pressures, she is less able or perhaps unable to provide a tranquil atmosphere that brings rest and relaxation to all. Perhaps we need to help mothers realize how valuable they are and how to feel truly fulfilled in their role. We need to find ways to make them less lonely and frustrated. They need to be relieved some of the time from continual child care. We think fathers are best for this. The children need them and they need the children.

There is no reason not to make use of an occasional baby sitter, relative, or friend to free both parents for something special, provided, of course, that their basic values and child-rearing principles conform to yours. Inconsistent discipline or negative values confuse the child and can undo much of your careful training in a very short time. A five-year-old girl told us recently that her baby sitter told her that a man might get her and cut her up in pieces. Before the child is able to reason, this type of information can be especially harmful. A little child like Pisha, whom we met earlier, will seldom understand the value of a $100 bill. But she does know the meaning of "icky." Those lessons which we repeat by our word and example will have the greatest meaning to the yet inconsistently reasoning child. So think twice about those care-givers and those institutions and those influences to which you surrender your child. And . . . about the possible unexpected and unacceptable meanings your little one may contrive from *your* own tongue.

CHAPTER EIGHT

The Creative Fives and Sixes

Danny comes racing into the house. You are half reclining on the divan, and in the middle of a telephone talk with Hilda Zielke, a new neighbor who has a personal problem and whose husband was recently appointed senior vice president in charge of the company division where your husband is employed. Danny, who has recently seemed to grow more slowly—his clothes not getting short so fast—has nevertheless become noisier than ever. And here in his wet, muddy little hands he has not one but two squishy toads which he can't wait to show you. Suddenly, as you try to listen to Hilda's urgent confidences, one of the toads spurts out onto your new blouse.

What do you do? It depends of course on your equanimity and your understanding of your child. But usually the best thing to say is, "Hilda, I have an emergency here with Danny. I'll call you right back." Then settle down to the fact that your five-year-old may be making up in curiosity for his other developmental delays while he is on a temporary physical height plateau. Be thankful for a lot of things: your blouse is permanent press, he can wash his own hands now, he can talk and listen well, and he doesn't mind a little scolding if you, yourself, are consistent, and he knows he is appreciated and loved. You are his best teacher.

Even though he now seems to be right-handed, his fine muscles are not yet well coordinated. So toads slip out rather easily, especially if he holds them as tenderly as you told him to the other day. Besides, haven't you wisely encouraged him to do things for himself at this age? Haven't you also admonished him to share, now that he is going on six? Isn't that what he is doing? And you are his best friend for sharing. Also, he is learning more with toads than he can yet learn by reading. He is not as clever as his sister was at five, but he is all boy. You are thankful that he is normal. And even if he *seems* excited because all the kids are going to school, he is far from ready for it! And . . . don't forget to call Mrs. Zielke!

By this time you or any casual observer can tell what kind of parents you have been. If Danny is secure, happy, loving, lovable, and obedient, with few, if any, eating or sleeping problems, you must have done most things right. Fortunately, there seems to be a happy leeway for some parental mistakes along the way without serious consequences, as long as the errors are not too basic. You realize Danny is pretty much a mirror-image of you since you have provided not only his inherited qualities but also the model after whom he has patterned his behavior.

If he does not have those lovely traits you cherished for him, it is still not too late for you to help him to change them, although it may be a great deal more difficult than it would have been before. The fact is that you will have to change first—change in your example and self-control. Don't be too proud or faithless to breathe a prayer for help. Read, for example, Proverbs 3:6: "In all thy ways acknowledge Him and He shall direct thy paths." Unless you use very tender, loving, firm, and consistent methods, you can do more harm than good—like breaking a branch when you meant only to bend it. The longer you postpone definitive training the more you will build hostility and the more danger there is that your anger and resentment will seriously alienate your child.

Candidate for Kindergarten?

By the time your child is five years old he has become quite a competent little individual. He can do most essential things for himself—eating, dressing, toileting, and speaking. Indeed, he is very bright! Some of your friends and family urge you to send him to kindergarten. He almost certainly will want to go, too, especially if some of his playmates are going. Social pressures—"everybody's doing it"—are alive and powerful at this age. The excitement of something that sounds so great is almost irresistible. And social pressure is often as hard on the parents as on the child.

Well, why not kindergarten? Here are some of our reasons why not: You must first decide your priorities. For example, few people would question the idea that physical health is more important than early education. The body is the battery for the mind, and your child's mental progress is largely dependent on his total physical fitness. So is the strength of his nervous system, his emotions, and even his moral stamina. School even for half a day at age five is not ideal from the health point of view. Until the child is eight or nine, he is especially susceptible to respiratory diseases. He needs to build up immunities to resist the germs to which he will be constantly exposed at school.

There are very few kindergartens that do not keep the children relatively confined in a classroom most of the time. Lack of physical exercise and the scarcity of pure air in the schoolroom are harmful to the lungs. Even with so-called modern methods of heating and cooling, many rooms admit little or no fresh air, especially in very cold or hot climates. The existing air is often recycled through the heater or cooler. In most homes there are relatively few people to take up the available oxygen which is vital to healthy lungs and maximum brain development. If the child has a long bus ride to and from school, the problem of excessive fatigue is added.

Reading-readiness workbooks and other near-vision academic work, as well as small-muscle activities such as printing, coloring, cutting, and pasting, are usually a large part of the programs. There are exceptions, of course; yet under normal circumstances there is no other way for the teacher to handle the number of children in her care than by a certain amount of regimentation and busywork activities. Her children must pretty well do the same thing at the same time or there would be chaos. Yet the children's eyes are usually damaged by too much close work, and the combination of pressures tends at early ages to make them nervous and high-strung. Manipulation of a pencil or crayon is still quite difficult at age five, especially for boys. The child may like to do such work at home, but there he is free to stop and rearrange his program at almost any moment, while at school he is more often expected to finish his assignment.

There would also be more flexibility—so desirable for the child of this age—in a home where there might be children of varying ages and the older could help the younger, with one set of family values rather than many sets as in a kindergarten. Children at home might also do approximately the same thing at the same time, but in general there would be more options for unstructured activities such as working together in cooking, cleaning, or other housework or gardening, going for short trips or walks, studying natural phenomena, marketing, or participating with their parents in whatever work they do.

We don't know enough about the actual physiology of the brain to understand clearly all the implications of its use in learning. Neurophysiologists cannot experiment freely with the human brain as they can with animals. But with the study and research they have been able to do, many neurophysiologists strongly suspect that cases labeled as dyslexic, perceptually handicapped, brain-damaged, or even mentally retarded are simply showing the results of unfair expectancies on the yet unready brain.

The problem of dilution of values is probably as important as the physical risk. When parents relinquish their parental responsibility to the school, even partially, they also give up their authority. Your child transfers much of his loyalty and admiration to his teacher and age-mates, who then become the examples he copies most. Since most of the examples are children, they dominate his behavior. Any alert parent knows that the life-styles of most children are not worthy of emulation. Your child has not yet matured enough to internalize his family values. He is still shaky in his thinking, not yet able to reason according to principle—to work out the basic whys of his conduct. It is often easier for him to learn the bad than the good. And the things he sees and hears are deeply imprinted in his mind. The acts he copies become habits that combine to form basic character for life.

Five- and six-year-olds need to run free as lambs, guarded and shepherded by their parents and fenced in where necessary to train and protect them. They should not be regimented into school-type tasks, such as "everybody does page 5 in his reading-readiness workbook, does the number exercise, or makes the letter K ten times." They should not be pressured to be socially accepted by their peers, to keep up with them in school tasks, and to compete with them for toys or teacher attention. These pressures are imposed not only by parents, teachers, and peers, but also by themselves in a struggle to maintain their self-concepts which are so very vulnerable at this age.

We are *not* saying that a child should always do what he wants to do when he wants to do it or that he should watch a lot of television or that he doesn't need boundaries and careful supervision. Your young child is a creature of routine and needs a predictable environment. Meals, nap, work-time, story-time, bedtime, etc. should be pretty much the same every day. He finds security in such regularity. This kind of program also subtly teaches important concepts of time, organization, punctuality, obedience, and self-control. If your child seems interested in signs or words or in writing his name, by all means help him, but do not allow him to stay at any close work more than about twenty minutes at a time or his eyes may be damaged. The eyes should not be kept at prolonged near focus when they naturally focus at a distance. [29, 41, 43]

The most obvious advantage of kindergarten attendance is that children learn the routines of school life and are therefore a little better oriented for the convenience of the formal classroom teacher in the first few weeks. Within a short time after enrollment in the first, second, or third grade, however, there is no noticeable difference between those who have been in preschool and those who have not.

A Real School at Home?

In many homes no attempt at school at all is needed. What children need most is time to work out their own fantasies in freedom and solitude, and to share home duties with you—which, properly handled, make very special play. Yet often when "all the other kids" in the neighborhood are going to kindergarten, the social pressures may get to your five-year-old, at least temporarily. A solution to this problem which almost always works out satisfactorily is to have "school" at home. In fact his school can be a better one than you usually find in an institution. This is presently working well in thousands of homes. Then the child need not lose face by being different from the other kids. He can truthfully say that he is going to school, too. If the other kids take their lunch, he can too, at least until he is satisfied that this is somewhat impractical. He could even walk outside for a ways and back to his "schoolhouse" if this pretending gives him satisfaction. It will not be a very much different program than what he has had all along at home but you will add a few ceremonies to give that special flavor of a real school.

Don't forget before-school chores. Making his bed, tidying up his room, as well as helping with the breakfast preparation and clean-up, are responsibilities a person should handle all through life before school or work. So why not start out right? Some major home tasks can come later but, the minimal morning jobs should be completed before "school."

Then set up a reasonably flexible program which fits into your household schedule and allows for individual interests. It may not need to be more than thirty minutes to an hour, or it could last most of the day, depending on your other demands. It should be at a regular time every day and not dismissed for every little intrusion that comes along. You could start with the flag salute, a patriotic song and a prayer. This is an excellent time for some spiritual training. Sing a song or two together, read or tell a story, preferably using some type of illustration, such as objects, pictures, or felt figures on a flannel-graph. Your child will not care for a lot of variety. These stories become like old friends when he hears them repeated. Sometimes let him tell the story. This helps him organize his thinking to get events in proper sequence. You may have to help him with questions, such as "What happened next?" or "What caused the problem?"

Something active should follow this quiet time—perhaps marching, hopping, tiptoeing, or skipping to piano accompaniment or records, varying the performance to the mood or rhythm of the music. Other musical activities are in the section ahead on *Making Music*.

Nature study should be an important part of your child's daily program. This may include working with plants, pots, or window boxes indoors, or a bigger garden outdoors; collecting, identifying and classifying leaves, rocks, shells, etc.; starting a nature experiment; or taking a walk to see what can be found to study. Your local librarian will be glad to help you. See the section on *Your Living Textbook* in the next chapter.

Don't ever worry about having a single-child schoolroom. Your child will be delighted to be the center of your attention and you will have no problem in sustaining interest. In your home you have the ideal teacher-pupil ratio even if you have more than one child. When a mother tells us that she sends one of her three or four children to kindergarten because she doesn't have time for all three, we wonder how much time she thinks the kindergarten teacher has for each child when she has twenty or more. In such a case the mother almost always loses a sterling opportunity to teach her child character lessons at home, yet surrenders him to the social contagion of other little kids before he has had a chance to fully absorb the immunities and priceless family values at home.

If you have an only child and feel so inclined, you may well take in another child or two whose family manners and values harmonize with yours. Some mothers do this as a means of a little extra income and feel they are using their time to better advantage. Although it is not generally necessary, some mothers feel that another youngster all or part of the time will help their own child to play and work with others more agreeably.

As a student, of course, your child should be able to clearly give his full name, address, telephone number, birthdate, and parents' first names. He should also know which is his right hand and which is his left hand. Names of the days of the week and months of the year should be familiar and soon become automatic. Be sure he knows or learns how to skip and how to pump himself in a swing.

Having Fun Indoors: Some Recipes

Outdoor activities should have first priority, but there are certainly many times when this is limited by weather or other circumstances. Also, since children at school have opportunities for art work and often make things to bring home, you may want to include some of this handwork too, at least for short periods of time. Have your child use chalk, *large* crayons, tempera paints with *large* brushes, and *large* paper. Support the paper on a chalk board, an easel, a table, or the floor. Do not use *small* color books and crayons or pencils at this age. They require too much strain on muscles not ready for fine control.

Fingerpaint is easy to make at home. Let your youngster help measure the ingredients and do as much as he can to help. Here are three recipes which can be made mostly with ordinary household materials. Find the one you like best:

Finger Paint No. 1 (makes 2 cups)

½ cup flour
2 cups water
1 tablespoon glycerine
1 teaspoon borax

Add enough water to flour to make a smooth, easy-to-pour mixture. Bring rest of water to a boil. Then add mixture and stir over low heat until thick. Cool. Add glycerine and borax. Add tempera paint or vegetable color as desired. Store in air-tight container in the refrigerator.

Finger Paint No. 2 (smoother; makes 2½ cups)

½ cup cornstarch
¾ cup cold water
2 cups hot water
2 teaspoons boric acid solution
1 tablespoon glycerine

Mix cornstarch and ¼ cup cold water. Add hot water; stir and cook over low heat until mixture boils. Remove from heat, add ½ cup cold water and boric acid. Add glycerine (makes it dry slower). Add tempera paint or vegetable color as desired. Store in air-tight container in the refrigerator.

Finger Paint No. 3

¾ cup laundry starch
1 pint boiling water
¾ cup soap flakes
¼ cup talcum
few drops oil of cloves or glycerine

Mix starch with cold water to make a creamy paste. Stir in boiling water until paste becomes transparent. Add talcum. When mixture has cooled slightly, stir in the soap flakes. Add oil of cloves to prevent souring. Store mixture in covered jars. When ready to use, add tempera paint for color.

The child at home who helps make bread, shaping it into various kinds of rolls and loaves, or who makes cookies which can be cut into different shapes, does not necessarily need playdough. (Louise Ames of Yale's Gesell Institute once told us that real homemaking is "three dimensional education" in contrast to the "two dimensional" experiences of school.[1, 2, 3, 25, 26, 27] Indeed, the best early schools, like the Waldorf schools, are much like home.) But since the "other kids" may have playdough at school, this is an alternate activity you may wish to use, especially in bad weather. It can be introduced when the child is as young as fifteen months, or at least as early as it can be kept out of the mouth. But it can be more creatively handled by age five or six. It is easy and cheap to make and keeps for several months when wrapped tightly in plastic in the refrigerator to be used over and over again. It can be rolled thin with a rolling pin, cut or formed into shapes, for instance, little houses, animals, or dolls. Pieces can be joined by dampening the dough slightly. For Christmas decorations, angels, bells, trees, wreaths, or stars can be designed. A bent paper clip can be inserted at the top for a hanger; then the shape can be colored with Magic Markers or paints and glitter. These will dry at room temperature or can be baked for an hour at 200 degrees. This speeds up the drying process and makes them stronger. Here is the recipe which a child can easily make:

Playdough A

2 cups flour
½ cup salt
About 1 cup warm water
Food coloring, if desired

Mix flour and salt well. Gradually add water, stirring first with a spoon, then with the hands, to make a smooth, stiff dough. Knead on floured board, working in more flour until the dough no longer sticks to your hands and is right to mold. Wrap in plastic and keep in refrigerator.

Playdough B

3 cups flour
1 cup salt
1 tablespoon vinegar
1 tablespoon salad oil
Mint flavoring for fragrance
Powdered tempera or food coloring

Mix well the flour and salt. Add vinegar, salad oil, and flavoring, and as much water as necessary to make a smooth, stiff dough. Store in plastic bag. This dough does not require refrigeration.

Thick liquid paint, used from squeeze bottles like hair coloring or shampoo containers, can also be made at home. This paint is a fascinating art medium. As it comes out in a thin stream, you can make pictures on heavy paper, styrofoam, cardboard, egg cartons, or paper plates. If desired, a comb, old toothbrush, or toothpicks can then be used to add a variety of textures. Set the creations aside for a day or so to dry. They become hard, raised, and glossy.

After the painting is complete but not yet dried, you can also make prints from it. Lay a piece of absorbent paper—such as a paper towel or plain or printed newspaper—carefully on top of your picture and smooth it gently with your hand. Then pull it off and you have a print. Sometimes several may be made, depending on the amount of paint used on the original.

To turn such prints into a kind of butterfly design, fold your heavy paper, open it again and make your picture on only one side but touching the fold. Then fold the paper again and smooth gently. This will duplicate the design as a butterfly's wings are duplicated. Here is the recipe:

Thick Liquid Paint

2 cups flour
½ cup sugar
12 cups salt
Wet or dry tempera or food coloring

Sift flour and mix in sugar and salt. Then add water gradually, using wire whisk or mixing spoon to mix until smooth and about as thick as batter for cake. Divide into small plastic bowls to add different colors. Pour a little of one of the paints into one squeeze bottle at first to check for consistency. In order for the paint to flow out in a steady stream, you may have to thin it or make the bottle opening larger. When the consistency seems right, fill the other bottles and start painting. To store, remove and wash the caps, cover the neck of the bottles with plastic wrap, and secure the caps again. Store in refrigerator. Before reusing, shake well, remove the plastic wrap, and replace the cap.

Sharpening Learning Tools

Sticks or straws in graduated lengths provide a challenge for the child. Start with ten of them cut in one-inch gradations from one inch to ten inches. Have him find the shortest and the longest pieces, placing them at opposite sides of his working space. Then ask him to place the rest in between according to size. Later you and he may make a set of twenty pieces with ½-inch gradations and a set of forty with ¼-inch gradations. A practical application of recognition of gradations in height would be dusting and arranging books of different sizes on bookshelves, grouping the books from smallest to largest.

Cutting pictures from old magazines or catalogues requires close work but may be used occasionally for variety. These pictures can be used to make scrapbooks or greeting cards, or collections of pictures can be used as collages to decorate a wastebasket or poster. Separate scrapbooks or sections of scrapbooks can also be designated for particular classes of pictures—food, wild animals, farm animals, pets, trees, people, etc. This gives practice in classification. Use blunt scissors at ages five and six, and have your child cut out the whole picture. Cutting around complicated curves such as heads, feet, and other small details is still too difficult.

Sewing buttons on cloth and a few stitches on a piece of cloth should be about the extent of the stitchery class. But stringing of beads, spools, or dry macaroni (perhaps dyed with vegetable coloring) helps the coordination of small muscles if you do not prolong the exercise. Shoestrings or ordinary string with the ends hardened by nail polish work well.

Sorting absorbs children's attention, especially if they must be in the house or if quiet is essential for any reason. If you have nails, screws, bolts, nuts, buttons or beans which need sorting, now is the time to get it done. As a means of keeping a child quiet in bed when ill, you may need to mix a few dried beans or lentils and rice, and/or other contrasting dried legumes or grains, or you can use two kinds of buttons to be sorted. This trains the eye and hand to work together and gives practice in seeing differences. The amount to be sorted should be adjusted according to the age and maturity of the child. The time should probably not be more than fifteen or twenty minutes for any close work without a change to distant vision or rest.

Colored sticks, even toothpicks, can profitably occupy a child for a while and are good for learning colors, developing eye-hand coordination, and encouraging the imagination. He can use these sticks to make geometric and other designs, people, animals, or houses on the rug or on a square piece of felt laid out on the table. The felt can also be the holder to roll or fold the sticks inside when not in use. They can easily be taken on trips or to the waiting room at the doctor's office. A sick child can use them on a tray in bed, or they can occupy several children in individual or cooperative activity, for example, with each one taking turns placing one stick per turn and seeing what comes out.

Five- or six-year-olds should do very little writing, yet they often want to write their names or certain favorite names or words. Although we see no harm in teaching them to do this, we warn again not to let them stay at any fine muscle task or close work for more than fifteen or twenty minutes. While you're at it, teach the letters correctly. (This might be a good time to reevaluate your own printing ability.) Do not teach a child to print in all capital letters. A copy of the manuscript letters which most schools teach in the first two grades will be found on p. 162.

Here is a little verse to make number writing fun and correct. Teach the numbers only as wanted or needed for practical purposes. They should be written the same size as the letters with a large pencil.

> 1—Straight down equals one.
> 2—Around and back on the railroad track.
> 3—Around and around once more.
> 4—Down and over and *down* once more.
> That's the way you make a four.
> 5—Down and around, put a line on top.

abcdef
ghijklm
nopqrst
uvwxyz
ABCDEFG
HIJKLMN
OPQRST
UVWXYZ

6—Down to a loop, and six rolls a hoop.
7—Across the sky and down from
    heaven,
That's the way you make a seven.
8—We make an S but we do not wait,
We climb back up to make an eight.
9—A loop and a line makes nine.
10—It's easy to make a ten, one and an
    O,
You have ten fingers, you know.
—*Anonymous*

Making Music

Even if you are not a musician, there are many things you can do with your child to give him a background of musical knowledge. Music has a strong influence on feelings and behavior, so it is important to establish a taste for a variety of good, high quality music during these most impressionable years. Children learn to like the kind of music they hear. Both the melody and the words of vocal music should uphold the values and attitudes you want your children to have. Rock and loud pop or disco music may damage a young child's nerves and his delicate hearing organs.

Records provide a controlled method of music education and are appropriate tools in the early program. To really know and appreciate a piece of music, it must be repeated consistently whether it is sung or just listened to. Simply playing music does not necessarily mean *listening;* it may become only background noise. A quiet time other than naptime is a good opportunity for real listening, for there are no other distractions. Encourage your child to imagine that the music is talking to him, and ask what the music tells him. For example, ask him if he gets a picture in his mind. He may like to draw or paint what he thought about or saw in his mind.

Children will not usually learn much before three years of age to carry a tune and to sing with a singing voice more than a speaking tone. They are more likely to gain this ability if you will sing to them from their birth. If your five- or six-year-old child or another for whom you have a responsibility is not able to carry a tune or if he speaks in a monotone rather than singing, there are several things you can do.

Get him to make some common sounds he can easily mimic from a record or from you. Don't make a point of his sour notes. Try a siren sound with an oo-oo, sliding from a lower tone to higher. Make the sound of the wind whistling around the corner of the house, the hooting of an owl or song of a bird. Repeat these daily as a game until the child "feels the tone" in his head and hears the difference in high and low tones. Also play an "echo" game to see if he can match the same single note as you with an oo, ah, or la. Stretch up tall for the high notes and squat down for the low ones. Let him originate a note for you to echo. Then go on to two, then three or more notes in succession as his skill in listening and imitating increases. Soon you have a tune. Rather than undertaking this kind of training in a formal-type of lesson, it is more fun for the child and you can achieve better results doing it incidentally while working with your hands, driving in the car, walking, or other compatible activities.

Sing songs wherever you are—at work and at play. You can also have a regular music time at story time or family worship, but keep your child close so that he can hear you clearly. A lyrical, clear woman's voice is often the best model; it is usually nearer to the child's voice pitch than is a mature male voice. If you have a piano to play, it will be helpful. An uncomplicated or even a one-finger melody is better than fancy playing to accompany children's singing, for it is easier for them to follow. Choose songs that are simple and childlike, and repeat them often enough to be well learned. Remember, children love and find security in repetition. In general, there should be no big intervals in the songs—jumping from low to high or vice versa. The range should be mostly within the octave from middle C to C above.

Never ask or allow a child or children to sing loudly. Yelling or the loud singing so often asked of children can damage the vocal cords, especially in young children. Unaffected, clear, melodious singing is the goal. If a varied sound is desired, sometimes have the child also try humming or singing through a comb covered with tissue paper.

Encourage your child to create music. He may add a new verse to a familiar tune, make up an original tune about an experience he has had, or accompany some of his rhythmic movements. Give him every possible opportunity to sing with the family, not only at worship time, but at almost any family togetherness time.

Let your young musician make a scrapbook of his favorite songs, illustrating each song with a picture. If the music is not available, just the pictures will do. Arrange opportunities for learning about different musical instruments—how they look and how they sound. A visit to a local school orchestra or band practice or concert, a music store, or whatever is available could be used as an introductory learning experience. Pictures of instruments are good reminders and can be added to the child's scrapbook. He also can and should learn to listen for the more easily recognized instruments in records or any music he hears.

He can begin to become acquainted as well with voice combinations—solo, duet, quartet, ladies' choir, men's chorus, and mixed voices: "There are two people singing that song" (or three, four, and so on). Commercial records that have a variety of nature sounds are available. All such identification at this age, however, should be strictly secondary to the child's enjoyment and appreciation of good music.

Help him to respond creatively to the rhythms of a variety of music. He can clap, march, tiptoe, gallop like a horse, sway like a tree, hop or fly like a bird. He can walk slowly or march briskly, in a circle or zigzag. Try arm movements, too, swinging them limply or stiffly, raising or lowering, and bending or straightening.

Together you can make and use an assortment of rhythm band instruments. Put a little rice, beans, or small rocks in a plastic "egg" or tube, a pair of plastic or foil plates, or other container, and seal with tape to shake like a maraca or tambourine. Use unopened ends of a large can or round heavy cardboard carton for a drum. Stretch rubber bands over a box with a hole in the top for a stringed instrument to pluck, or make "cymbals" with foil pie plates and spool handles. Even bells to ring or sticks to hit together make a pleasant percussion sound with music.

And try a rhythmic tapping or clapping game, similar to the game Follow the Leader. You go clap-clap-clap. Your child goes clap-clap-clap. You go clap-clap, rest, clap-clap, rest; he repeats the pattern. Soon your budding musician can initiate the rhythms and you follow him in a cycle of turns.

If you want your child to really learn about rhythm, at first use your instruments only with familiar music which has an even beat. Eventually, you can have him learn to clap or "play" only on the accented notes and "rest" or soften the beat on the others. In ¾ time he will *play*, rest, rest; *play*, rest, rest, etc. And in ¼ time he will play on one and three and rest or soften on two and four—*play*, rest, *play*, rest, etc. He will also learn to clap or play softly for *pianissimo* and louder for *fortissimo*.

Let your youngster blow across the tops of bottles of different sizes and listen to how the pitches differ. Have him also strike the bottles gently with a stick or spoon. As he becomes more pitch-conscious, try filling bottles, glasses, or jars with various amounts of water to produce several pitches. These can then be tapped or blown across to make simple tunes. This musical-glasses activity can become more complicated as he grows older—using more containers to produce the full scale and make possible more difficult melodies.

But don't start instrumental lessons. The same principles apply to readiness for formal music lessons as apply to school-type tasks. Save your effort and money for the most efficient learning time, which for music seems to be at eleven or later. A national sampling of 1500 professional music teachers found a consensus that age eleven and a half is the best time to begin—usually well after a good start has been made in school learning.[62]

The Kitchen Laboratory

For your child there is much mystery and magic about the kitchen. Its learning experiences are almost limitless, unless, of course, your biases deny the kitchen its spell on your youngsters. Participation in cooking, baking, and other food preparation will teach much about sounds, tastes, smells, and textures. It will take longer and require more patience than sending your little one out to play or turning on the TV for him, but will bring you a great deal more happiness and satisfaction and make yours and your child's years ever so much more productive.

One Sunday while sitting in our living room in Japan, I was startled by an excited voice from the kitchen.

"Look, I did it, I did it!"

"Did what?" I asked.

"I didn't spill a drop."

"Kathie, what are you doing?" I yelled at our five-year-old homemaker. Caught temporarily with office papers over and around me, I couldn't easily jump to see the spectacle. Dorothy was teaching a class.

"I'm pouring honey into the honey thing. Come 'n' see . . ."

Sure enough, she had spilled nary a drop. Dorothy had had her practicing pouring, first with water, then with birdseed, then with flour and salt, and later with juice and milk. Kathie had learned the use and the fun of a funnel to fill narrow mouth bottles or cans, and to clean out leftovers and put them in smaller containers. And now she had mastered honey!

". . . All by myself," she stated, and with a reasonable pride.

As your child helps you measure cups of flour or fractions of cups of other ingredients and cuts halves or quarters of food items, he also learns mathematics concepts. When he puts eggs in the refrigerator tray, he can learn what a dozen is as well as the necessity for careful handling. And setting the table teaches him to count silverware and plates. He finds out by experience that some foods are heavy and some are light. When he puts away groceries, he learns to classify and organize. He exercises his memory and the ability to see differences as he helps put things in their proper places. In handling utensils, he practices small muscle coordination. To watch bread rising, gelatin hardening, waffles baking, and vegetables becoming tender after he helps prepare and cook them are all exciting educational experiences.

Watch for simple recipes he can make alone or with minimal supervision. Let your young apprentice cook have the satisfaction of planning and preparing a simple meal for the family as soon as he is able. This is often done by well-trained six-year-olds and sometimes by fives. Teach him how to help with meals for company, waiting on the table while you visit with your guests. He can even help with the shopping. Let him make a picture shopping list either by drawing or by cutting pictures from magazines so that he can help by "reading" his own list.

Help your child see the value of refrigeration by leaving out a little milk in a covered container and watching what happens. If you process any foods for winter storage, let your child participate in the preparation and process of canning, freezing and drying. Dry some grapes in the sun so that he will know how raisins are made. In a blender whiz up two or three sliced frozen bananas with an equal amount of frozen berries and enough orange juice to blend for a healthful dessert—without added sugar. Serve it in a cone or sherbet glass and call it a "smoothie."

You can fill out his knowledge about food values, balanced meals, and nutrition along with kitchen activities. For example, when he scrubs potatoes for baking, he should know that eating the skins gives us more of the special vitamins and minerals to build up our bodies. Explain: "That's why we get them clean enough to eat." He should know that his bones, teeth, muscles, and blood are built from the food we eat, and the better the food, the better our body. Participation in food preparation often sparks interest in learning to like a variety of good food. One little girl we had in our home had a serious distaste for tomatoes, or thought she did, until she was allowed to pick one from our garden, wash it, and cut it with a small sharp knife for her lunch. Somehow the dislike vanished.

Kitchen Gardening

Besides being a simple and pleasant indoor learning activity, kitchen gardening has the advantage of no weeds to pull or bugs to contend with. The top inch of carrots, radishes, turnips or beets will grow leaves when set in a shallow dish of water. Also the top inch of pineapples will grow in a pot of moist sand for a few weeks and then should be transplanted to soil. A sweet potato suspended with small end down in a glass jar filled with water and placed in a sunny window grows into a beautiful plant.

And, of course, there are avocadoes. To get the big avocado seed to root, it must be suspended with the large end down in a jar of water and placed in a dark place. When leafy shoots appear, it can be planted in soil. Other no-cost items to plant in pots or cottage cheese cartons are orange and grapefruit seeds, peach or apricot pits, and wild nuts and seeds.

For an especially simple and quick experience in watching seeds grow, put a moist sponge in a saucer filled with water. Sprinkle the sponge with grass seed or bird seed and keep it moist. You will have grasses in three to five days.

Probably the most exciting activity of all is sprouting seeds for food. If you haven't done it before, you will be delighted, too. Point out that as the seeds sprout and grow they make better and better food. The amazing part of such a project is that, after a day or two, the nutrients of the sprouts are several times greater than those of the seed itself—Vitamin C and B complex, minerals, and protein. It seems that as the seed germinates, part of it is changed to these elements to make the other part grow. Explain to your child that the sprouts are better than the seeds for his body, to make him big and strong. In fact, sprouts are easily digested, quickly absorbed by the blood and are low in calories. They can be used plain or in salads, sandwiches, stews, omelettes, casseroles and Chinese dishes, or, when lightly cooked, as a vegetable.

Show your child how to grow sprouts: Place seeds in a wide-mouthed container, e.g. a quart jar. Cover with net or cheesecloth secured by a rubber band. Almost any kind of natural seed can be used except tomato seeds—which are poisonous when sprouted. When we say "natural," we mean *not chemically treated;* treated seeds probably would not sprout properly and might make you sick if they did and you ate them. Alfalfa seeds, mung beans, lentils, and wheat kernels are the most popular and usually the easiest to grow sprouts for eating. Soak 1 or 2 tablespoons of seeds in water overnight. The water should not be chlorinated. Drain and then rinse them with fresh lukewarm water and drain again. Put them in a warm, dark place such as a closet until the sprouts are the desired length. Keep the seeds moist, but not wet, by rinsing them two or three times each day, tilting the jar at an angle to make sure all the sprouts are rinsed. A couple of hours before using or refrigerating, put your sprouts in indirect sunlight to develop green color. This signifies the presence of chlorophyll, a valuable blood builder.

Just one more thing to add: Beans and peas should sprout one and a half to three inches long before harvesting, while lentil sprouts are ready at about one inch. Grain sprouts should be only as long as the seed, except for alfalfa, which can grow until you see tiny green leaves. For sunflower and sesame seeds, as soon as the sprout starts out of the seed it is time to harvest, if you don't want a bitter taste. In any case, the big gain in nutrition occurs as soon as there is any visible sprout. If you have trouble remembering to rinse your sprouts several times daily, write yourself a note and put it by the kitchen sink, or just cover the equipment with a dark towel and keep it close by where you will see it often. But share this responsibility with your child. Ask him to help you remember. Teach him to use an alarm clock if necessary and to be dependable in its use.

The good spirit of cooperation and habit of obedience you have already established will greatly facilitate such kitchen projects. Be sure to teach safety rules as well as be watchful about them.

Children at five or six can learn to use knives and other rather dangerous equipment properly. You will need to plan on some spills and breakage, but be patient. Skill, like Rome, isn't built in a day.

Creative Little Individuals

Curiosity is as natural to the young child as it is to a puppy. How you as parents use your power to stimulate or squelch this quality may determine how creative your child will be not only in thinking but also in using his muscles and his sensory skills—taste, touch, smell, vision, hearing. Highly curious children tend to be more creative than less inquisitive children. From the time your child shows a desire to explore, he should be given as much leeway as is practical and safe. This is a special opportunity for you because you normally have, or should have, the sole privilege of the impressionable early years. It is a terrible sacrifice to miss them. As curiosity is carefully fostered, the child will become more interested in his environment and more motivated to find out about it.

Yet as with other abilities, curiosity should not be forced. If overstimulated by too much newness, or by adult-inspired fantasies, your child may become hyperactive, insecure, or even frightened. Especially when very young, the child prefers familiar people and places, with new objects gradually introduced in the context of the familiar. This is one of the great dangers of early schooling. As an alert parent, you will want to watch for signals and provide neither too much nor too little.

As the child grows older, he will become more interested in new people and places. Probably more important to him than any other one thing will be your warmth, consistency, and responsiveness in revealing your attitude toward his learning. If you are inquisitive and use source books to find answers to your questions and to gain more information, he will take note and imitate you.

Supplying too much information too soon, especially facts to learn by rote, deprives your child of discovering facts for himself by experiment or observation and tends to limit his curiosity. He needs to find out many things for himself—to experience real events and explore concrete objects. He gains real understanding only of what he observes firsthand. This is one of the great damages from television. It does sometimes instruct him but usually when it does, it keeps him from actively investigating his environment. This is especially true in the fields of science and math, which involve thinking and understanding rather than just facts. The emphasis in early childhood should be more on constructing things than instructing about them.

In general, the child's curiosity for the new is aroused by way of what he already knows. Don't rush him from one activity to another. He needs time to redo his activities so that he can develop confidence in learning a particular skill. These repeated experiences become a part of his store of understanding. And he needs opportunities to experiment in various situations, to develop his skills with gradually increased difficulty as he matures. This valuable quality, which a relatively stable home in the child's first eight or ten years can provide, is something a school can seldom offer. Schools in general actually tend to squelch a basic bent for creativity, for their high pupil-teacher ratio cannot adequately accommodate individual interests.

Still another advantage the home has over usual school conditions is that children feel free to ask more questions when they are in a small group or when alone with an adult. Encourage their questions and ask some yourself. Be careful not to ask many questions that simply require rote answers. Rather, ask questions that stimulate thinking and require solutions to problems, summarizing or evaluating, like "What do you think would happen if . . ." or "Can you guess? . . ." or questions asking *how?* or *why?*

The child's learning will not necessarily proceed at a regular rate. At times he will develop so fast as to be spectacular but again he may seem to be on a developmental or learning plateau. This probably means that he is concentrating on organizing what he has already learned—a necessary preparation for further learning. One characterization of the young child's development is that it is predictable but will go steadily by jerks. Don't be concerned if you see him staring off into space occasionally. Daydreaming or deep thought is often necessary and is a positive trait at this age as he works out his fantasies.

If children are not often inventing fantasy games and experimenting with their own ideas, it usually means that they have been entertained too much, either by television—which has already been shown to stifle imagination—or by overscheduling with trips, lessons, and too many playmates.

The other day we read an article in a church magazine by an early childhood specialist. She was moaning that busy mothers need a half dozen grandmas to run their errands and pick up the pieces: to stop and shop, pick up the kids from nursery school, kindergarten, piano lessons, tumbling team; for baby sitting, answering service and as entertainer grandmas. And grandmas are just great. Besides, older people need a challenge, don't they? We asked several of them.

"Why the gym and piano lessons, nursery school, kindergarten, and constant obsession with shopping?" asked one.

"Is she particularly restless?" another inquired.

We didn't think unusually so, for we knew the author.

"I feel sorry for her," the third said, "but not because she has so many errands. Why doesn't she just settle down and make a home?"

"Does she have to work?" the first asked.

We doubted that, knowing her very capable husband.

"Maybe she has a bug about women working," the third grandma suggested.

"She had better decide," said the second, "if her job is more important than her kids. If it is, I'm glad I'm not the grandma. . . ."

"Why is it," interrupted the first, "that mothers these days—all adults for that matter—think that they have to provide all kinds of lessons and fantastic experiences for their youngsters? Why don't they just love them and let them be, give them a chance to grow up in the nest where they belong?"

When we first read the article we thought it might be a considered suggestion to occupy older people who have time on their hands. The grandmas in fact admitted that they would be glad to do a few errands if the children were well-behaved and nested down at home and mother were tending to her mothering business. But they weren't about to give up their retirement to cope with hyperactive youngsters and substitute for a mother whose career meant more than her kids.

The fact is that these grandmas were not only instinctively right but scientifically sound. Parents must realize that little children have plenty of imaginings of their own, that a warm family is quite the best socializer, and that unless the mother's absence is one of urgent necessity, she should be at home, instead of depending upon adult-contrived entertainment to occupy her children. Generally the child who spends more time alone or with adults tends to be more creative. Genius has been shown to thrive with a great deal of parental warmth combined with ample opportunity for solitude. Agatha Christie, one of the more successful writers of the century, still had been allowed no formal lessons at nine. Her affectionate mother was convinced that the best way to bring up girls was to let them run, to give them good food and plenty of fresh air, and not to force their minds in any way.

Activity should be produced *by* children, not *for* them. They need to use their own ingenuity to devise interesting activity. All parents need to do is provide an atmosphere of encouraging cooperation and have things around for them to use in spontaneous construction and play. Most of us would call it junk—various kinds of boxes, scrap lumber, other raw materials, tools, etc. Such relatively rough, inexpensive equipment—nails, boards, cans, rocks, sand—usually holds the children's attention, promotes language practice and ability, and increases creativity to a far greater extent than store-bought toys. Imagination is suppressed by overindulgence in ready-made, detailed toys that can do only one specific thing. The best toys are relatively simple and can be used in various ways as the imagination of the child directs.

We were fascinated one afternoon when visiting a couple and their young son. With a little help from his father, he had constructed a large, flat box with divisions in it which he called a "zoo." He had collected a variety of plastic animals from cereal boxes, and he and a friend played quietly for an hour or more in a corner of the room while the adults visited. When alone, he sometimes played with a make-believe friend. In another home we admired a homemade dollhouse—curtained, draped, and furnished by a child and her older sister. One family made a "city" out of small cardboard boxes painted to look like buildings, and they had several plastic cars that could be driven through the "streets." Such activities are especially useful for bad weather days when the children cannot be outdoors very much.

The fact is that with few exceptions, manufactured stories on TV and toys in the stores tend to curb a child's natural development. Most of them have limited use. Tales from your own life; a garden; a hammer, nails, and a little waste lumber combine well with a child's imagination to build great understanding, neat farms, and beautiful castles.

Dorothy and I often grinned at the sight in our backyard or sometimes on the living room floor. Out there was Dennis in a plastic fireman's hat with a piece of garden hose and his little red wagon or scooter. Day after day he "put out fires" all over the place. Imagined fire, imagined buildings, imagined water. It was master pantomime by an imaginative novice. We discovered that helping with a key item was all he needed. Usually it was a tool or hat. A captain's hat, and he could make a boat out of his wagon or a cardboard box or even a neatly stacked lumber pile. An army hat and he was a sergeant or a general; a band with a turkey feather and he was an Indian warrior; a baseball hat and he could use a stick and a ball or can or acorn to become a big leaguer. Our garage was his laboratory. Everything in the house and yard was a toy.

Dressing up in adult clothes, rearranging chairs to make a train or covering them with a blanket to make a tent or house, playing store, playing house, or imitating any grown-up activity, gives expression to the children's ingenuity and inventiveness. Such fantasy is their way of dealing with reality. It seems to be a factor in increasing their concentration and perseverance at tasks and in building self-control. It prepares them to work more skillfully with

you around the house—cooking, washing, ironing, sewing, cleaning, repairing, marketing, and gardening. It also better enables
them to cope with anxiety and frustration, for indirectly it helps
them handle life's problems.

Though a certain degree of order and neatness is essential in a
home, it is good for children to have a place where they don't
always have to put *everything* away before bedtime or whatever.
Mothers who sew or fathers who do woodwork usually like to leave
their work so that they can pick it up where they left off. Play in
progress by the child—building a railroad or a toy—may often be
the same. The continuity will encourage persistence and concentration on his "task."

Parents can sometimes participate in children's "pretend" play.
They can also encourage the child to imagine what animals or birds
would say if they could talk, or to look at the shapes of clouds and
think what they are reminded of in the way of animals, people, or
things. The attitude of parents toward such fantasy makes a
significant difference in the degree of imagination a child has.
Play-acting is often a valuable teaching tool for parents in
preparing the child for some event or change in his life. It can
sometimes help in discipline when roles are reversed temporarily—
as when daddy does the dishes and mother goes out to a meeting.
One family used this idea by occasionally having each member sit
in a different place at the table and adopt the role of the usual
occupant. This opportunity to see oneself as others see you was
designed to improve the mealtime behavior and atmosphere,
which it remarkably did.

Building Speech Skills

Even though young children develop a rather impressive vocabulary by the time they are six, it does not mean that they have
full understanding of the significance of many words they hear and
use. Usually they give only one meaning to a word and that is the
literal meaning; for example, they may understand sick, but not
heartsick, or they may have an idea about "splitting" but not a

"splitting headache." They are not usually able to deal with figures of speech, idioms, symbols, or abstract words such as "she's a peach," "out of hand," "Yankee," "air pocket," or "fishy." This accounts for the innocently funny remarks they make which bring much amusement to adults. Most children do not achieve the understanding of double meanings of a word until they are eight or ten years old or older, as, for example, to be able to give a correct answer to the question, Why is a blackberry red when it is green?

Almost all young children do a lot of repeating of sounds or words in normal speech. They do not yet have an adequate flow of words to express their ideas, especially when they are excited about something they saw or did. This may be exaggerated even more when they are trying to talk to someone who is disinterested, distracted, or preoccupied.

Serious stuttering or stammering are nervous speech disorders—as contrasted with lisping or cleft palate problems, which are mechanical in nature. You can forestall such nervous problems by providing, as much as possible, a simple, calm, quiet environment that does not get on anyone's nerves, including your own. Generally you set your own pace and pressure by your choice of involvements, so try to organize your home wherever and whenever you can to avoid conflict and tension.

The same factors that cause other maladjustments, such as dyslexia or loss of motivation, also tend to cause most speech disorders. Learn to give reasonable time and attention when your child has something special to report. In any case, never unnecessarily draw attention to his speech problem or discuss it with anyone in his presence. Time and avoidance of pressure, anxiety, and criticism will usually enable him to outgrow this particular difficulty. If it is not corrected or becomes worse, see a qualified speech and hearing specialist.

Relaxation and proper breathing are important for good speech development. When things get a little "high" or out of hand in the home, suggest that you both lie down on the floor and pretend to float. Close your eyes for a few moments and pretend you are drifting in a quiet pool. Then pretend you are blowing out the candles on a birthday cake, breathing with the diaphragm from the lower chest, but not noisily. At other times, quickly make and blow a pinwheel to make it spin, or blow up a balloon. Panting like a dog with a huh-huh-huh sound is good for relaxation and proper breathing as well as for emphasizing enunciation.

If your child has difficulty with some sounds, think of some way to emphasize that sound in an informal way. For instance, use the coughing sound for *k*, "la la la" for *l*, horse neighing for *n*, rooster crowing for *r*, steam escaping for *s*, the clock sound for *t*, wind for *wh* and buzzing bees for *z*. In some cases it may be necessary to demonstrate how you place your tongue, teeth, or lips in making a certain sound, as for *f*, *j*, *s*, *th*, or *l*.

Special Learnings

If you have been alert to the practical needs of your child and have followed the suggestions in this book, your five- or six-year-old will have already mastered some of the skills noted below. But we will list here a few things we have not mentioned before:

Sometime soon your "pupil" should learn how to tell time, starting with a home-made paper-plate clock with large numbers and movable hands. Have him learn the hours first, then the quarter hours, and finally exact minutes. He can learn, when your electricity goes off temporarily, to check the correct time by radio or telephone and reset all of your electric clocks. He can also change them when there is a statewide time change to or from daylight saving time.

If your "kindergartener" has not yet learned the ABCs—how to recognize them and know many of their sounds—and this worries you, try teaching them to the tune of "Twinkle, Twinkle, Little Star":

A B C D E F G,
H I J K LMNOP,
Q R S and T U V
Double U and X Y Z.

Now I've said my ABC's.
Say them with me, if you please.

You can sharpen your child's hearing discrimination by helping him recognize and name the rhyming words in verses you read to him or having him supply words to rhyme with one you suggest, such as hill (bill, kill, fill, mill, etc.) or bat (hat, cat, fat, sat, etc.). He should also develop the ability to hear and suggest words which begin like *bear* (bat, bug, big, boat) or *funny* (fig, fall, four, fiddle). You can do this as a game while traveling, walking, waiting, resting, or during routine working with your hands.

Learning to describe a person, object, or living creature by shape, color, size, and other characteristics is excellent practice for developing vocabulary and speech skills. Make it into a guessing game between your child and you—"I'm thinking of something that is little" (or big or green or red or soft or rough, or clean or dirty, etc.). When the younger ones can understand classifications, you (and later, he) can say, "I am thinking of something." He asks, "Animal, vegetable, or mineral?" You say, "Mineral," and finally he correctly guesses, "The big rock in the front yard," or later, perhaps, "The Rock of Gibraltar."

If the pets in the family are for the benefit of the child, but not necessarily for protection or for the satisfaction of others, it is better for the child to wait to get his own until he can take the main responsibility for its care. A dog of appropriate size and temperament is much more of a companion than smaller pets, but if your location makes this impractical, he can find a little animal friend such as a gerbil, hamster, or turtle who needs and depends upon him for its sustenance. Or, you may want to let him select a fish or bird to care for as his responsibility.

Teach your youngster to be a good host or hostess. Give him practice in making and acknowledging introductions properly. Play-act this with him until he understands that he should say the name of the older person first and then present the younger, pronouncing the names plainly. Encourage him to smile and shake hands—firmly but not wildly—without prompting from you. Your warmth and hospitality to guests or your response to visitors, of course, will be among the most practical and meaningful lessons he can have. Practice in thinking of others is the best therapy a child can have for shyness, which is usually self-consciousness, and which, if allowed to flower, may encourage a selfish disposition.

When we were employed in school administration, it was not only our duty but our privilege to have many guests in our home. Our children loved visitors and were always interested in whoever came. Our four-year-old, Kathleen, was a born hostess. She was often the first one to greet a guest, take him by the hand, and lead him to the sofa. Then she would invariably crawl up beside the newcomer with a book to show and tell. At that point we often had to tenderly restrain her or she would have taken over with more books and questions. We usually distracted her by asking for her "help" in the kitchen. We could not allow the entertainment to revolve around her even if people were charmed by her loving ways. We are gratified that she never outgrew these outgoing hospitable gestures.

We remember how she would sometimes shock a guest with, "Let me take your shoes off?"

"Why . . . er . . ." the guest was usually nonplussed.

"Everybody takes off his shoes," she would admonish. And truly in Japan we did not wear shoes indoors. Yet most foreign guests did not know this and we hesitated to insist on the practice for such visitors. But not Kathleen. What was good for one was good for all—kisses, hugs, sitting on your lap, or taking off your shoes. Discrimination is not the talent of a young child, yet her motives must not be put down.

Stretching Your Child's Horizons

Though the home environment is sufficient for early exploration, at five or six it is time to widen your child's world, especially if you have not done so already. As he grows older, he is able to observe and learn more. Make a visit to a farm where there is a variety of animals, or to specialized farms such as a dairy farm, chicken farm, fruit, vegetable, or grain farm. Some city children have little understanding of the source of their food.

Watch how a home in your community is being built so that your child discovers how the wires bring the electricity and the telephone into a house. Let him see the heating ducts as they lead to the various rooms from the furnace and the pipes which lead to the water faucets, and others which take oil or gas to the furnace. Then show him as much as you can about his own house or apartment—the electric meter and fuse box, any visible wires, pipes, ducts, or the furnace.

Occasional trips to visit the post office, fire department, police department, city government offices, a local garage, bakery, or a manufacturing plant will expand your child's understanding of the community. We hope the father can be the instructor for some or all of these trips. Make them as thorough and educational as is appropriate for fives and sixes.

If your child has not already visited the library, it is time to begin to do this quite regularly. As occasion arises, perhaps on a holiday, vacation, or other family outing, take a trip to the zoo, the aquarium, the natural life museum or other special exhibits. Don't miss the airport and train or bus depot.

No doubt your child has already been introduced to the supermarket. But have you involved him in it enough to make it a progressive learning experience? Or do you let him sit in the cart for a ride just to keep him out of mischief while you get what you need and check out? Letting him choose his favorite cereal is hardly an educational hurdle.

Shopping actually involves planning for balanced nutrition, money management, selection of quality products, decisions on quantity—a mental exercise which, over the years, you have developed but may not have analyzed for its complexity. Talk things over with your preschooler even if you think it is over his head. Discuss food values, and let him help you as much as he can. Perhaps he can handle the discount coupons, identified by their pictures, and he can easily spot favorite family brands of canned or packaged foods.

Camping is another excellent family togetherness activity that children of this age especially enjoy. Share the planning, packing, and all the camp chores with your youngster. Help him learn to follow a hiking trail, to use a compass, interpret a simple map, and to carry his share of the responsibility. Observe the trees, plants, streams, birds, and animals. Ask him to "teach" you. He often will, in fact. Learn about the homes and family habits of the wildlife and compare them with his. Teach the need and value of preserving our natural resources by precept and practice. Show him how to put out the campfire properly and leave the campsite cleaner than he found it. Even if you live in the city, your child needs to learn how to protect our environment by doing his part to prevent land, water, air, and noise pollution.

Making Moral Youngsters

Character is formed in progressive stages and is based largely on intelligence, ability to postpone gratification, and ability to maintain attention. A great psychology professor taught us in college that a person is measured by his willingness to sacrifice present pleasures for future benefits. In general, your child's character development progresses at the same rate as, and is closely related to, his perceptual and reasoning ability. The great privilege of parents is to take the newborn baby who has no understanding of social or moral behavior and train him to have a true conscience with high principles.

As we suggested earlier, the baby arrives without habits, prejudices, or even a conscience. He must first learn to trust someone to love and care for him. Preferably this is his parents—or consistent parent substitutes, not a variety of care-givers. The sense of trust thus established determines the basis of trust in a higher being, his God. Along with this he must learn to delay his wants and learn to obey—important early character traits. It might be called *love* and *limits*.

Until he is able to reason consistently—in the age range of late sevens to middle elevens—your child will tend to imitate and adopt the character traits of those around him. This places key responsibility on you to provide his main examples. He can learn cooperation, kindness, and other socially acceptable standards of behavior best by copying those who exhibit these qualities and desire to develop them in their children. This also accentuates the risk of allowing him to play with other children, especially those who are not carefully supervised and controlled.

Because he does not naturally have any practiced principles or consistency, his parents must provide the authority that helps him know what is right and what is wrong. His reasoning ability should be nurtured gradually by helping him to understand why certain behavior is best. He needs to learn to consider the rights and feelings of others and gain some understanding of the consequences of his acts. He should be allowed to make decisions beginning with choices between two acceptable alternatives. This helps to develop and strengthen his sense of values. He should be given opportunity to think and act for himself on the basis of principle as much and as fast as he is able. Gaining approval for good behavior is a powerful incentive to the child in wanting to continue desirable actions, for he tends to repeat that which brings him satisfaction and happiness. But normally until he is nine, ten, or eleven years old he will not become fully aware of the meaning of rules and the reason for them. Only then can he really understand them in relation to the principles on which they are based.

Character or moral values will achieve the most complete stability when they have a sound religious base. The idea of a God who made us, redeemed us, and wants to take us to heaven to live with Him in a perfect place is a powerful motivation for character development. Teaching about a loving Jesus Christ can begin very early in life, not with the thought of earning one's way to Heaven but rather to return the Father's love by trying to do what He knows best. Little children respond readily to approval by their parents, and the approval of God is an added incentive.

The child forms his concept of God by the relationship he has with his parents. He will picture God as the kind of person his parents are. If he is threatened, slapped, yelled at and scolded, he will think of God as having these qualities. If they are kind, loving, forgiving and patient, he will know the true attributes of God.

Five- and six-year-olds have a rather limited understanding of prayer, although they begin to be aware that this can be a solution for problems. Seven- and eight-year-olds see prayer as talking with God and asking him for things, while after nine years of age or more, children feel that they can actually have private and personal conversations with God.

The church nursery, kindergarten, and primary age groups can be a delightful educational experience for a child. Though the subject matter has a spiritual emphasis, the music, stories, and verses or fingerplays usually take into account the child's developmental needs. Usually the parent attends with the child or is nearby and can learn the songs and get ideas for worship times at home.

Even though your child may attend church every week, he will enjoy a special visit during the week to get acquainted with the church building without all the people in it. Walk with him quietly to look more closely at the choir loft, the pulpit where the minister stands, and the organ or piano. Perhaps you can even have a short visit with the minister in his study. Respect for the minister and reverence for God are key factors in developing self-worth. After all, your little one *is* a child of the King!

Work is a particularly valuable character-building activity. It challenges one to accept responsibility and to persevere even with discouragement. As the opposite of idleness or excessive play, it absorbs aggressive energies in a useful direction and keeps body and mind profitably occupied so that there is little time or inclination for negative activities. It promotes purity of thought, exercises the intellect in planning and develops such character qualities as thoroughness, industry, responsibility, and dependability. Most children can do much more work and take much more responsibility than parents require. Carried out consistently, this concept can make child-rearing one of the world's greatest long-range pleasures instead of the plague so many parents have found it to be.

The TV Temptation

Some believe that television is second only to parents in influencing values in young children because it comes so early in life and in such great quantities. Averaging twenty-four hours a week for preschool children, television occupies very large share of the child's waking hours. Certainly it vies with other little children in transmitting its contagion. TV violence has been clearly shown to cause antisocial behavior in children. They absorb and imitate what they see and hear, and often they reproduce, partially or wholly, aggressive acts to which they have been exposed. Yet TV is something parents can control if they will. And it is vital to sound child-rearing that they do.

Even if you shield your children from violent scenes, television incurs a very real detachment from real life and has a distinctly negative effect on the child's socialization. When you take him off into adult-contrived fantasies and absorb him with silly or absurd dramatic scenes before he has learned to reason or become accustomed to normal, *everyday* life experiences you warp his value system—at a time you should be refining and stabilizing it. We have already noted the uselessness of reading fairy tales, some of which actually strike fear in many children.

Skilled observers are worried that TV is turning children's minds to mush. It replaces constructive work or play, teaches passivity, stifles creativity, and instills a low tolerance for the frustration of learning. After viewing sugar-coated lessons presented with show business gimmicks and entertainers, children are easily turned off by tasks that require only minimal effort and self-control. Even many so-called "educational programs" such as "Sesame Street" reduce rather than lengthen the child's attention span because of the rapid changes in theme. Much of this learning is premature and meaningless. It is convenient for a child to know his ABCs when he reaches school age, but he has little use for them at three or four.

Because children are notoriously gullible, believing almost

everything they see and hear, the commercials create in them wasteful, even dangerous wants for many things, including un-healthful foods and unnecessary clothes, pet foods and toys, before they have developed the reasoning ability to resist. One concerned specialist commented that we are on the way to becoming a nation of "sugar junkies." Some of the breakfast cereals, for example, are 40 percent or more sugar, and many of the most popular flakes and crispies are so refined as to have very little food value. Recently one prominent physician-nutritionist, commenting seriously about a highly TV-advertised breakfast food, said that the box had more actual nutritional value than its contents. And another stated that TV ads may be "permanently distorting children's view of morality, society, and business." He found that by the time children are twelve years old, many find it easier to decide that all commercials lie than to try to decide which are true.

Someone might question, "Don't you think children need to know what goes on in real life?" We must be quick to answer that indeed a child must ultimately know the realities of life in this world. But everything has its time and place. In the child's early years, he should be shielded from unnecessary corruption until his reason is well developed. It is not necessary for him to personally participate in drugs, alcohol, murder, rape, robbery, and other violence in order to know "what is going on in the world."

CHAPTER NINE

The Reasoning Sevens, Eights, and Nines

On a cloudy day not long ago we were flying from Houston to Dallas. My seatmates were Marshall, age seven and a half, and Kelly, age eight, two bright sons of professional couples from Dallas and Houston. As we approached Dallas our plane had to drop through thunderheads—great billowing, cumulus clouds. The turbulence at first shook up the young lads and then they turned to conjecture about what "the clouds are made out of."

"Steam," said Marshall, confidently.

"No," corrected Kelly, "clouds are snow."

After several minutes of speculation they saw water appearing on the windows and allowed that it was "really rain." I asked them where rain came from. "It comes from God," Marshall replied.

"But how?" I questioned.

"He pours it out," Marshall answered.

"How do you mean?"

"Like out of a big pitcher, I guess."

"No," Kelly corrected again, "He bangs the clouds together."

"Then how does He get rain out of snow?" I asked.

"I don't know."

Marshall's and Kelly's ability to reason consistently from cause to effect had not yet caught up with their healthy curiosity.

A few moments later, Kelly shouted, "Look, we are almost touching the ground."

"Yeah," Marshall agreed.

We were still flying at about 5,000 feet. The captain had just

189

announced 6,000 feet and given us seat belt instructions for landing. The boys had seen buildings and trees and signs of life as we lowered through the clouds but at their ages they still had little idea of distance or space. Their eyes were becoming ready for near and far vision and they were trying to reason things out. But few children, especially little boys, can reason consistently until well after seven or eight. They still have problems answering how or why.

But reasoning is beginning to flower at these ages, along with self-evaluation, understanding of time, distance, space, use of money, sense of humor, and other factors important to quality learning. The child still feels warm toward adults, yet reaches out for peer approval, although still with more enthusiasm than judgment. He is learning the meaning of fairness and is developing group consciousness while acknowledging individual differences. He is also developing small muscle coordination. His eyes are readying for near work, his lungs are developing fully, but his heart is subject to strain. And, son or daughter, he or she needs more than ever the friendship of Dad.

Tools for Learning

An enormous amount of research has been done in the last twenty years on the development of young children, particularly on the maturation of the senses. Unfortunately a great deal of this research has not been brought together and applied with common sense to the education of the young child, especially where it concerns formal schooling. Yet the only avenues of learning are through our senses. From the time your child is born he is drinking in sights, sounds, tastes, smells, and textures in the process of discovering the world in which he lives.

It is impossible to keep him from learning as long as he is in touch with life. But it is also impossible to hurry up his learning, except by making available to him in a quiet, gentle way—mostly by example—that knowledge and those experiences which are appropriate for his development. Formal schooling or similar stimulation so highly touted by a few psychologists can be almost as damaging as outright neglect.

No matter how bright your child, the maturity of his senses dictates his ability to learn in a quality way. Yet educational trends in this country have gone beyond the perception limits of most little children, leaving in their train high percentages of school failure, drop-outs, delinquency, and crime. It is not until the late sevens to the eights, nines, and sometimes the tens that the senses—hearing, vision, taste, touch, and smell—seem to come together in the maturity required for efficient formal learning.

Taking Time with the Senses

We advise that you not rush your child into any formal learning before he is ready. For example, hearing-readiness, or auditory perception, is, like all of the senses, closely related to age, and seems to occur a little earlier than visual maturity. This may be one reason that researchers suggest that young children seem to learn better through hearing even than seeing, and hearing perception is probably even more important to reading than visual readiness. Sounds must be heard accurately in order to be identified or reproduced accurately, so it is important that you speak slowly and clearly to your child. The ability to articulate speech sounds goes hand in hand with hearing discrimination and perception. Both are usually achieved by the age of eight or nine years. In speech, as in other development areas, boys may lag a year or so behind girls.

While the eyes—visual perception—often develop a little later than hearing, about the age range of eight to nine they are mature enough easily to distinguish differences in letters and move from line to line and adjust to reasonably large print. Before that time children often have difficulty with reversals, such as *d* and *b*, or *saw* and *was*, and there are other problems with eye movements. You have perhaps already noted that your five- or six-year-old will often follow the lines with his fingers, while your eight- or nine-year-old has sufficient visual coordination that he doesn't have to "read with his fingers."

Leading eye researchers—ophthalmologists and optometrists—insist that prolonged looking at books, near objects, or even confinement in a room without enough opportunity for distant vision often cause "myopia," abnormal nearsightedness. Young children are normally far-sighted, but being forced to adjust at too young an age to near objects over a period of months and years actually causes the immature eyeball to be wrenched out of shape. Anxiety is believed also to contribute to this abnormality. It has been observed that the incidence of myopia is reduced when children are mature enough to do the work expected of them without pressure.

A number of psychologists and vision researchers such as Francis Young[65] and William Ludlam[38] along with such clinical ophthalmologists as Henry Hilgartner[29] and Frank Newton[45] have done thousands of vision studies. They conclude that even keeping children confined for periods of several hours a day within the four walls of a classroom may induce myopia, especially when combined with close work with books, easels, and blackboards. Dr. Young's work proving this theory with monkeys was criticized by some, but there was less criticism after he reported his study of Eskimo families. In Point Barrow, a few years after Alaska became a state, the children were required to go to school, beginning at age six. Although both their parents and grandparents had virtually no myopia, up to 58 percent of the children in some schools had myopia. Alaska is now permitting later entry.

And we must remember that the process of perceiving and organizing and reasoning out the words and sentences are much more complex than just seeing. This is why we say "visual or auditory perception" and "cognition," instead of simply "seeing" or "hearing" and "reasoning." It is not the eye alone that must read the words on the page, nor the ear alone which hears; the brain also must bring meaning to those words by association with other knowledge and past experiences.

The right hemisphere of your child's brain should have experience and understanding, for example, about time and space and distance and direction before pressures are put on his left hemisphere to put together typical academic skills. School tasks require the analysis, integration, and synthesis—the bringing together and right mixing—of visual information. For normal school-type learning, the brain must reach a certain degree of maturity before it is ready for this sustained coordination of the senses.

If even one of the senses—vision, hearing, touch, taste, smell—is underdeveloped, formal learning to that extent is handicapped. The senses must work closely together and depend much on each other for the most efficient and effective learning. Thus what we call "intersensory perception" is important, and it is not mature until all senses are ready. Yet when the two senses generally considered the most important—seeing and hearing—become equalized in their function at about the age of nine, children will usually learn quite well with relatively little stress and strain.

Before this maturity has been reached, regular schooling has negative effects even beyond poor achievement. It often brings apathy on the one hand and rebellion on the other, or both. The results are generally poor attitudes toward school and general maladjustment. True, the child who begins his schooling with deficient perceptual development may have the tools, but they simply are not yet well-tempered or strong or sharp enough to do the job. What we are asking him to do is like trying to flip over a pancake with a piece of foil or trying to shave with a paring knife. He may eventually get the job done, but it will likely be frustrating and possibly be botched in the process.

Such a child does not generally catch up in achievement even after his physical development is complete, for the premature pressure has already damaged him both emotionally and physically. And for many children this immaturity lasts into the eights and nines. We have already pointed out that some cases of so-called "dyslexia" or other "minimal brain dysfunction" are likely caused by nothing more than such pressure on the unready organism to function beyond its ability.

The development of the delicate mechanisms of the brain is still largely a mystery, especially in relation to learning. One reason is that researchers cannot experiment to any great extent upon the human brain as they can on animals, and another is that the child's brain is altogether higher than the animal's. The child has the potential ability to reason and worship—something animals cannot do. And the physical health of your child's brain is completely dependent on the basic health of his body—on exercise, diet, sunshine, fresh air, rest, temperance and abstemiousness—as well as a balance of study, work, and relaxation.

Your child is capable of memorizing and of absorbing many experiences and facts in an informal and natural way, as he gradually matures. But until there is maturity and communication or integration among all the various senses, we know that formal school-type learning is an overload and almost certainly will hurt him. This damage is likely due not only to maturation and coordination of the perceptual processes but also to nature's way of assigning certain tasks or dominances to the two hemispheres of the brain. On these assignments depend many aspects of learning. And we now know also that the division of activity between the two hemispheres of the brain is not usually well established before the age range of eight or nine.[39]

It is true that, when read to by their parents, most children learn to read well, and some children seem to learn to read by themselves. Generally, they are motivated by the interest in books demonstrated by their parents or older brothers or sisters. In many cases of precocious reading ability, an older brother or sister did much to teach the little one to read. There seems to be no reason to squelch this ability as long as the child does not strain his eyes by too much adjustment of his eyes to his book. About twenty to thirty minutes is considered the longest "safe time" for your child to read at this age, provided that he gets outside or to the windows where distant vision opportunity is immediately available to him when he is through.

Such spontaneous reading ability often is obviously developed without pressure, competition, or coercion of any kind and so avoids many of the dangers of school-type learning. However, in such early reading children do not always fully understand what they read. Yet their comprehension improves as they grow older.

If a child asks to write his name or wants to learn what certain printed words say, tell him. But first emphasis should be put on good language usage as a part of your parental example, and on your parent-child companionship in work, play, and other everyday home and community activities.

Becoming Reason-Able

We have frequently referred to a child's ability to reason. This development is closely related to the physical maturation of the senses and also the structure and function of the brain. Through years of close observation and experiments with young children, the influential Swiss psychologist, the late Jean Piaget,[48, 49, 50, 51] came up with some very interesting and significant findings about how children think. These conclusions have been checked out by many other researchers and have been found to be valid.

He determined that the ability to understand a certain physical law is a sign of maturity in reasoning power. This is the well-known law that mass is constant—always the same—regardless of its arrangement or changes in shape. He relates this understanding to the law of *conservation of energy*. It is evidently *not* something that can be learned until a child is mature enough. It has been found to bear close relation to readiness in beginning school tasks. The age range for understanding this law is from about seven or eight to eleven or twelve.

The experiments to assess such reasoning ability take many forms. For example, you can try this experiment on any four-year-old. Show him two short, stout glasses of water the same shape and size and filled to the same levels. Ask him if there is the same amount of water in both. Of course, he will say "yes." Then, *while he is watching*, pour the water from one glass into a taller, thinner glass. Now ask him if there is still the same amount of water in both. Often five- or six-year-olds will answer that there is more in the tall container (because they see that it is higher). A seven or eight-year-old will generally tell you that the amount is the same regardless of the shape.

Recently an interesting couple joined us at dinner with their five-year-old boy and six-and-a-half-year-old girl. Both children were thought "exceptional" by their parents, and indeed they were very bright. We tried the glass and water experiment on the little boy while his older sister watched. He responded as expected, saying there was more water in the taller glass. We then asked his sister, knowing that she was not only older, but also a girl, and had had more time to think it through. But she gave the same answer.

Later we tried a similar Piagetian experiment, taking two equal piles of ten pennies (or you can use candies, or beans, or other convenient item). We asked them to count out each pile and verify that each had ten. We then spread one pile out into a line about eight inches long and left the other as it was. When we asked the five-year-old if the two groups still had the same number of pennies, he said, "No, there are more in the stretched-out line than in the pile." This time his six-year-old sister hesitated. She was not sure, and was therefore revealing some growth in such concepts, although a seven- or eight-year-old would normally realize the groups of pennies still contained the same number.

The parents looked on, astonished. We decided to try just one more, this time a story which tests a child's understanding of motive or reason, with implications for moral values. We told them about little four-year-old Jimmy and his big sister, Sue. Jimmy was angry when his mother would not give him dessert until he finished his vegetables, so he smashed his glass on the floor. Sue felt very badly for her mother and bent over to pick up the pieces, but in doing so, she knocked off *four* glasses! Who was the naughtiest, Jimmy or Sue? The four-year-old unhesitatingly answered, "Sue." "Why?" "Because she broke the most." To the parents' surprise, his sister agreed—showing typical inconsistency of a young child at this transitional stage of development. But some sixes and most seven- or eight-year-olds would normally recognize that the intention of Sue was good and therefore she wasn't naughty at all.

These are simple illustrations of the reasoning ability of young children. They serve to explain why until now many of your parental explanations of "why" have not seemed to satisfy them. This does not mean that you shouldn't tell a five-year-old *why* he should not, for example, go into the street or climb up on the neighbor's garage roof. We need to try to help children understand cause-and-effect relationships—the causes and likely results. We should give them experiences that will develop their reasoning powers. But we do need to recognize their limitations and not expect them to think like adults.

Few parents appear really to understand this need. Occasionally our children's thought processes will astound us, and their clever ideas will make us feel they are super bright. And they may be. But we must never forget that they are not very consistent in their reasoning, and that serious damage can be done to children by urging them into tasks or situations or institutions requiring mental tools that are simply not yet strong enough or sharp enough to do the job.

Rivalry Problems

Competition for young children as experienced in school can be damaging to their self-concept. The evidence is most noticeable until they reach the age range of eight to ten when their increased maturity, self-worth, and ability to reason helps them cope better with the inevitable ups and downs of school life. In fact, in the early grades rivalry has been found to make children mistrustful, suspicious, and destructive. They do not know how to relate to "opponents" who are supposed to be their friends.

Overzealous parents sometimes urge their young children to become interested and involved in competitive sports. They may have Little League or some other special activity in their community or relate to young athletes performing well on television. They see a great potential for their offspring to participate and perhaps excel. Perhaps they first need to know all the havoc that can be caused with shattered nerves, damaged emotions, and other maladjustments such pressures can cause, even for the winners, but especially the losers. Though the child of seven, eight, or nine generally has much energy and apparent strength, his heart is not fully mature and he can easily overexert himself or become overly fatigued.

Much is said about building good interschool or even international relationships and good sportsmanship through competitive sports. Yet competition not only puts undue emotional stress on the young child, but it also has a negative effect on his values. Although there are exceptions, research indicates that the majority of athletes show little interest in receiving support and concern from others, little need to care for others and little need for close attachments. This often seems to be the type of personality necessary to gain victory over others.

Competition for time or distance in underwater swimming—an exercise children of this age often try—is especially dangerous. We recall an experience of Dorothy's in rescuing a young boy from drowning. He had determined to swim the length of a rather shallow pool underwater. He breathed deeply a few times and dived under. Dorothy swam along on top to keep pace. Suddenly she noticed that he rolled over on his back and stopped swimming. She could see bubbles coming out of his mouth. Though not entirely realizing the seriousness of the situation and regretting having to spoil his fun, she pulled him out. He was blue in the face, but recovered quickly in the fresh air. We afterward learned that this is not unusual. Hyperventilation, or over-breathing, alters the body chemistry, depressing the urge to breathe. Low blood oxygen results before the swimmer feels the need to breathe and can cause unconsciousness without warning. Many deaths occur even in guarded pools because the unconscious person may continue to swim. Since he is underwater, no one is aware of his problem.

What Next?

After we have presented the reasons for later schooling we are usually confronted with the question, "What should we do for our child at home if we don't send him to some kind of school? Shall we get him a correspondence course?"

Research shows clearly that the greater the child's store of experiences and knowledge before he goes to school, the more successful he will be in school and in the future. Parents are usually the best ones to help him build this background of information—but *not* through book learning as such. Children learn best by the discovery method—by doing, experimenting, observing, and imitating—not once over lightly, but repeatedly.

There is a tendency to think that children must gain most information and education by reading it in books. Book learning certainly has value when it comes at the appropriate time, but there is plenty of knowledge that can be accumulated by the child without his having to decipher symbols in order to find it. The less effort consumed in the process of learning to read, the less it will detract from other intellectual growth.

Almost all the activities suggested in earlier chapters can be continued and expanded as the child's capacity increases. But a number of additional suggestions are presented here:

Some physical proficiency may be helpful before school entry, particularly if entry is in the age range of eight or later. Much depends on the school your child will enter. While we don't suggest sports for sports' sake, we believe it wise to minimize differences in skills. Become acquainted with the games played at school. If ball playing is popular, coach and practice with your child—as exercises in coordination—enough ahead of time so that he can catch, throw, and hit reasonably well and knows the principal rules. He might need a basketball backboard or basket mounted on the end of the garage or another place away from windows. Or you may provide for skills in skating, jumping rope, and similar activities.

Give your child practice in following and constructing simple maps. This involves knowing left and right; the directions of north, south, east and west; and the ability to give instructions to someone who may need help in finding a place he is familiar with. Give him practice in being the "navigator" when you drive. Get him acquainted with the globe—the continents, the oceans, and special places significant in current events or family interests.

You should help him learn about the customs, geography, and dress of people from other countries, both from stories read or told and from actual contact with people who have lived there, whenever possible. If there is a family of a different race in your neighborhood or church, invite them over. Ask them to wear their native dress and perhaps bring some pictures or mementos of their homeland. You might be invited back to share a typical meal of their nation. Simple costumes and food of other lands can be prepared for special learning times at home with pictures or family souvenirs gained from former travel.

Don't forget your homeland—its distinctive customs and places. With all its faults and troubles, it is still important to your child. It was fun teaching our children how to draw maps. First we started with rooms in our house, then with houses in our block. Next we plotted our way to church and the park, then to the post office, fire station, and bank. The children drew pictures of these places. They became not only familiar with our town, but the maps were quite symbolic, real pieces of art.

By this age children can begin estimating distances and better understand concepts of space and time. And there is an important thing many parents forget these days when it is popular to ridicule our government: Be sure your children appreciate their country. Help them understand the true meaning of freedom and our responsibility to help maintain this freedom by insuring the rights of all people—at home, at school, or on the highway. Instill pride, loyalty, and patriotism by your example and the opportunities you provide. See as much of your land as you are able; learn about its heritage in stories, museums and historical places. Sing songs about it, watch patriotic parades, and display its flag proudly. Love it, respect it, care for it, and help preserve it. If the ship of state sinks, we all go down with it.

Your Living Textbook

Nature is an unfailing source of children's curiosity and delight. Greater understanding of the awesome detail of our marvelous universe emerges strongly with the beginnings of consistent reason-ability. It was no doubt implanted in us by a Creator who knew the best way for young children to get acquainted with Him. Nature provides opportunities for limitless exploration and observation: the weather; the starry heavens; the environment of the pond, stream, lake or sea; growing plants and trees; the many creatures of the earth. Simply introducing some of the many opportunities to learn is all that is necessary, for the young child's program should not be highly structured in the first eight to ten years.

A walk or an outing is always appropriate. It can be the take-off point for many learning experiences even within most cities. Any bud, flower, or rock might spark the child's interest. Then it is your responsibility to fan that spark into a flame by your interest and encouragement, but not by pressure. Such enrichment enhances your child's quality of life, not only for the present but also for all his future. It is a delight to him from a very early age. You do these things with him for fun and inspiration. The learnings are incidental as together you share your discoveries.

If you can secure a large calendar with partially blank squares for each date, you can use it for a weather calendar. Or, you and your child can make one so that the daily weather conditions can be recorded—mostly by little pictures drawn by hand. You might illustrate the types of clouds, sunshine and rain by boots, umbrella, or streaks for raindrops and a zigzag line for a lightning storm. Use some specific words as you talk about the weather, like fog, drizzle, mist, hail or sleet. A simple gauge, such as a flat pan, can be made to measure the rainfall. Notice the signs of evaporation on the sidewalk or street after a rain by observing what eventually happens to the puddles. Perhaps there will be steam rising from the pavement or from a roof. Chart the time of sunset and notice whether the days are getting longer or shorter.

You can also record the high and low temperatures. You will need a large, easy-to-read thermometer, preferably clocklike. If you have access to weather forecasts, you can compare them to what actually happens as well as use them to plan what type of clothing to wear. Even adults are not always very realistic about the outside temperature when it varies considerably from the inside. At this age be sure to take your youngster into this planning.

Some simple study of astronomy is often appropriate for the seven- or eight-year-old child. Phases of the moon can be observed and constellations identified. Study the movement of the sun around the earth and how it brings seasonal changes. Learn about and watch the effect of the seasons on the trees and wild life. Measure shadows at different times of day. Children's books from your local library can supply information you do not already know. And there might be a nearby observatory or planetarium you could visit. These are exciting and highly profitable expeditions.

If you do not consider yourself to be a naturalist and perhaps are even somewhat squeamish about worms, bugs, or frogs, you may need to do a little adjusting. With a little practice and determination you can be smart enough to suppress your feelings when your child's curiosity leads him to want to touch or experiment. Just have him keep his hands away from wild rabbits, squirrels, and similar animals that may be carriers of rabies.

The simple information you already have is enough to start with. Numerous children's books are available either at your library or can be obtained inexpensively at nearby book stores. It is important that the information you provide be accurate. Once you glimpse some mysteries of creation, you will probably become a nature-lover yourself. Work on this, especially when you are sharing it with the excited, sponge-like mind of a youngster you love.

Equipment for nature study usually depends somewhat on your locality and the particular interests of the family. Many parents are already rock-hounds, shell-collectors or bird-watchers, and children will quickly participate. An inexpensive pair of binoculars or a small telescope is about as complicated as you need to get. In fact, an ordinary good magnifying glass will bring an entirely new and exciting dimension to ordinary objects.

Look through the lens at a bit of moss, seaweed, grains of sand, a shovelful of sod with soil under it, snowflakes or tiny blossoms. Magnified under a lens, they reveal exciting secrets not visible to the naked eye. Oftentimes, just lifting up a board that has been lying on the ground for awhile will expose a colony of interesting worms and bugs. And if you ever have the chance, try underwater viewing in tropical or semitropical waters for out-of-this-world surprise and excitement. You can use either regular snorkeling equipment or any home-made waterproof box or can with a glass on the bottom which can be partially submerged in a shallow tide pool to give you a view of the garden, fish, and coral under the sea.

Enchanting the Senses

Your child's senses—his eyes, ears, nose, tongue, and skin—are like little antennae reaching out to absorb the sights, sounds, smells, tastes, and textures of his world. As those senses are developed through his repeated experiences and observation, they are forming a background or context into which he will fit his problem-solving tools in the future. The fragrance of blossoms, for instance, appeals to the sense of smell even from babyhood.

By the time he is about seven or eight, sometimes before, your child will be fascinated to inspect tiny blossoms under a magnifying glass and try to count the separate little flowers. On one large stem of Queen Anne's lace (a wildflower) about three or four inches across, a naturalist friend recently counted nearly fifty separate stems of about fifty little flowers each for a total of more than two thousand tiny blossoms. But just because we smell or count them does not mean they should be picked to wilt and die. Teach respect for growing flowers, and perhaps pick one—or at most only a few— to put in a vase. Such respect and control are important related learnings. Call attention to the pungent odor of newly cut grass or hay, the salty ocean air, or the special scent of evergreen trees, to alert your child to what he can identify by smell.

The handling of various living creatures should always be done with careful supervision for the sake of the creature and your child. You will need to know what is safe and what is not, and he will need to be coached to learn tenderness and care. Squeezy mud, spongy moss or lichens, slippery sand, and water also have their fascinating part to play in learning by the sense of touch. Let your child gather and feel such textured items as pine cones, feathers, bark, cotton, and various nuts and seeds. These can be used in artistic creations for rainy days indoors.

Learn how the seeds travel. Throw dried maple seeds into the air to see how they spiral down like little helicopters. Watch how the wind carries dandelion and other such seeds like little parachutes through the air or how some stick to your clothing or catch on the fur of animals so that they are scattered to start plants in other places. Look for seeds floating on top of the water in a stream, pond, or lake.

Sounds of nature may fall on deaf ears unless they are tuned to them. The time to tune them is in the early years before they are desensitized by the artificial sounds of modern life. Children are thrilled to learn how to identify bird songs, night creature sounds, the many moods of the wind, and the pounding surf. Such exercises are very special in training the ear to discriminate.

Colors, especially in nature, nearly always attract a child's attention, so be alert to opportunities to enjoy them. On rainy days watch not only for the gray hues in clouds but also for rainbows in the sky. On sunny days show your child a rainbow through a water sprinkler, or in a soap bubble held up to the light, or made on white paper by the sun shining through a prism or reflected from the beveled part of a mirror. At this age he will begin to understand that light thus broken up into its parts makes these colors, and without light there would be no colors at all—just like at night. Watch sunsets and sunrises from a variety of places— across a body of water or from a valley or a mountain or hill. Find opportunity for enjoying the color of flowers in parks, gardens, or florist shops. Best of all, plant your own flower garden, a little here, a little there, outside or inside your apartment or house.

Some Special Pets

To many adults, worms are not especially attractive creatures, but youngsters are usually charmed. The work of worms will be much more valued if you and your child make a wormery and see how they pulverize the soil and help things grow. Fill a gallon glass jar with alternate layers of soil and sand. Plant grass seed on the surface of the soil to keep it cool and moist. Because worms like dark places in which to work, cover half of the jar with black cloth or paper. Before adding about ten worms, watch them and touch them to see how they move and feel. From time to time remove the black paper for short intervals to see how the worms work and live. Watch how they change the profile of the soil layers in your jar.

An ant farm can be made in a similar way except that you should fill your jar only half full of soil. With a shovel dig up an ant hill and carefully put it on top. Then cover the dirt with cotton and sprinkle it with water every few days. Ants will need to be fed cookie or bread crumbs, and honey or sugar water. They, too, will work best under the black paper which you can remove occasionally to watch their work and "community activities." After a week or two put the ants and dirt back where you found them.

Spiders make enchanting study. They are really not so scary as they seem, as long as you know which are poisonous and which are not. They can be watched in a jar with holes in the cover for air, a piece of damp cotton or sponge for water and insects for food. Help your child preserve the web of a spider by spraying it thickly with white shellac and then pressing a black cardboard against it. This delicate and artistic creation can then be covered with clear contact paper.

Every child should have the experience of observing the life cycle of a butterfly. Pick up a caterpillar or two and some leaves from the plant on which you found it on one of your nature walks. Put them in a jar covered with gauze or net held with a rubber band around the jar rim. Keep the caterpillar well fed with fresh leaves until he makes himself a cocoon. Then it is a matter of patience— watching and waiting—until the flying creature comes out and is set free. Some find it fun to keep a picture record of these happenings.

Then there are tadpoles from a creek or pond. They can grow up in a large bowl filled with water from their own home locale. It should be changed once in awhile with water from the same source to provide its own natural food for the growing creatures. Many other small animals and insects can also have temporary lodging in a large ventilated jar while being observed by your family.

And, even in the city, try to have a bird feeder, especially for winter. The feeder can be a plastic milk carton or jug cut out on one side and hung on a tree. It may also be a simple wooden tray or other feeder attached or hung outside the window sill, or a special little wooden house on a post with a device to let down the food gradually.

If you have squirrels which steal all the seed, you will of course have to invent a method to keep them away. Since at our home we have hickory, oak, and black walnut trees which provide plenty of food for the squirrels, we keep them off of our bird feeder. We secured an inverted open gallon can on the metal post of our feeder so that the squirrels cannot get past it. After a few frustrating attempts, they learned not to try. We always keep a pair of binoculars nearby to get a closer look at our feathered friends, and we also have bird books to identify strange or new visitors.

An Economy Garden

Information on regular outdoor gardening is so plentiful that we will not go into detail here. It is a highly worthwhile learning activity for your seven-, eight-, or nine-year-old. And when outdoor gardening is impossible either because of the weather or because a little plot of ground is not available, windowsill gardening remains an important experience that should not be omitted. Notice how plants respond to the sun, growing and turning their leaves toward it. See how you can make them develop equally on all sides by turning them one-quarter turn each day. Try putting a plant in a dark closet a few days and see what happens—becoming yellow or dying. Also notice the similar effect when you do not provide enough moisture for a plant, or sometimes drown it with too much water.

Many plants can be rooted from simple, small cuttings taken from larger plants in your house or your friends' plants. Put them in water a few days until they develop enough roots to transfer to a small pot of soil. Others may need wet sand in which to root. But a little effort, care, and attention can have you in a little forest of plants in a short time with little or no outlay of cash. A terrarium made with miniature plants in a glass jar or jug takes the least maintenance of all once it is made. Sometimes these plants can be wild ones you gather in the woods.

Learning about the Body

Don't forget the marvels of the human body both in structure and function. Knowing how and why things happen the way they do provides a good background for taking care of this valuable machine. By this age your child should understand the importance of good food—like high quality fuel in a very expensive, but irreplaceable automobile. See that he appreciates consistent health checkups, and make sure he practices cleanliness in all that he does.

He can learn the names of some of the bones and how together they form the skeleton of the body. He can learn what happens inside the body to the food he eats. Use a balloon to help him understand what the stomach is like and a rope or long soft hose to resemble the intestines. A rubber band will help to show how a muscle works, a sponge to illustrate the lungs, though you should explain that the lungs mostly soak up air rather than water. A bicycle pump or air compressor at a service station can demonstrate the pumping action of the heart. Teach the child how to find and count his—and your—pulse, first at rest and then after running. Have him compare the rates, and also check his and your number of breaths in a minute. And teach him simple first aid.

In discussing the function of the blood, explain that a special amount of blood goes to the part of the body where the activity is taking place. For example, after he eats and his stomach is full, a special amount of the blood goes to that part of his body to help digest his food. If he runs or swims, the blood goes to his arm or leg muscles. If he's just finished eating, it can't help his food digest, so he might get stomach cramps. That's why we don't swim immediately after eating. We can't think too well or study when our stomachs are full, because our brains need extra blood for this, but the blood is too busy helping with the digestion of our food. This is why our minds work better when we do not keep our stomachs working except for our regular meals.

Take a thumbprint by rolling the thumb on a stamp pad and then on a paper or card. Examine it under a magnifying glass. Help him understand how very special he is—that no one else has a print exactly like his. Let him know that this is not the only way he is unique. His differences in appearance, his ways of doing things and his thinking make him one of a kind, very valuable to his family and to God. Let him make a design or picture with as many prints as he wishes to make.

The Nobility of Work

The vital principle of physical work is as old as creation. God gave it to man as a positive means of character development. Work requires a sense of responsibility, dependability, organization, and a certain degree of diligence and skill which help to develop both mind and body. It also demands patience and persistence as well as encourages neatness and orderliness. Along with the feeling of satisfaction and personal worth in having done something of value, these are factors that cannot be so well developed with any other substitute. Other qualities built by constructive physical work include industry, ingenuity, self-reliance, economy, integrity, courage, strength, firmness, leadership, independent thought, and common sense—all urgently needed today.

Unfortunately for humankind, we have invented ways to lessen our work time and the amount of physical energy expended in work. Then we have substituted sports and amusements, many of them passive, for active work. Industrialization and mass education also have brought about more use of the head and less use of the hands. This imbalance has seriously diluted the quality of our society. Work with the hands has been shown to be necessary for emotional health. It has also been used effectively as therapy for different types of neuroses and other physical and mental illnesses. Dr. Karl Menninger, one of America's leading psychiatrists, has repeatedly told us that garden therapy is one of his most effective treatments for mental problems.

Certain learning advantages inherent in work are not so easily acquired in other activities. It is a rather mysterious but established fact that mental ability is increased in about the same proportion as the ability to use the hands increases. Performance of systematic chores at home almost invariably carries over to good study habits at school. As the child works, he discovers that things must be done in sequence. He has had to do this in dressing himself— undershirt goes on before outer shirt, and socks before shoes. In work, such planning is intrinsic in achieving efficiency. Gardening, for example, requires the soil to be properly prepared before seeds are planted. And in painting, in most cases, if you don't start at the *top* of your project, you will spill paint on the part you have finished at the bottom.

By the time your little worker is seven, eight, or nine, he should be quite a proficient helper. He should know he is a valued part of the home team and can share in almost everything that needs to be done at home. And he should be rewarded with authority to the extent that he can take responsibility. As long as he is not overworked, he should be kept profitably busy doing as much as he is able. In most cases, this should still be with one or both parents. And its value extends beyond the obvious. At the same time the hands are occupied, you and your child can share confidences, talk over his frustrations, discuss values and practical lessons. None of this can ever be so profitably handled in a more formal setting.

Practical skills which both boys and girls of this age can learn are how to change a tire on a bicycle or change wheels on a car, change the oil, put water in the battery and some even learn to adjust jump cables for emergency starting, including all the safety precautions that must be observed. They can learn to repair or replace broken electrical fixtures or plugs on lamps and appliances. They can fix leaky faucets and squeaky doors, polish silverware or shoes, and mend, or wash and iron clothes.

Also, now that many paints have a water base and therefore are not so much of a nuisance on clothes and skin, your child can paint a fence or other simple outdoor object as a preparation for more complicated painting jobs later on. This is of course best done with you working at his side. Woodworking also can be an ongoing project with increasingly difficult construction as practice brings skill. Various crafts including basket-weaving, knitting, and crocheting—for either boys or girls—for short periods are valuable skills, and far superior avocations to rivalry sports.

All these activities involve safety principles. The necessary rules should be clearly taught and the project carefully supervised until the child can use tools and machines safely.

Children should be encouraged to work energetically and efficiently—not with slow, lingering movements, making a long job out of a short one. Your example while working with them is crucial here. A reasonably high standard of excellence should be expected—whatever is worth doing at all is worth doing well. But it is wise for both you and him to be realistic about what he is capable of doing. At these ages—as with their ability to reason consistently—there may be as much as several years' difference between children in their maturity and readiness to do fine muscle activities. If your child has trouble finishing something that is too difficult for him, help him to follow through to completion. But resist the temptation to finish it for him. He needs to avoid the habit of leaving projects unfinished.

The Money Manager

Arithmetic, including decimals and fractions, is simply the symbolic representation of real things. If children can first build up a store of knowledge from dividing and measuring, as in kitchen and garden experiences and in the actual use of money, school math will seldom present any obstacles. A weekly allowance, the amount determined by you, is probably the best way to start. Some parents make the allowance depend upon points earned by certain good behavior and jobs done. However, this could be misunderstood by the child to mean that chores or behavior have monetary value. So we lean toward viewing the allowance as a sharing of family income, just as work is the sharing of family responsibilities. Good behavior and satisfactory completion of jobs are something you as parent can expect from your child without pay or other material reward. Payment for special projects or as summer assistant to you or your spouse might be exceptions.

Make handling an allowance a valuable learning experience. Teach your child carefully, for money involves responsibilities and obligations. If it is used selfishly or wastefully, it will actively teach selfishness and waste. Depending on the point of view of the family, show your child how to divide his allowance into four parts, let's say—preferably even into four containers (or three or five, or any other number, depending on your plan): one for savings; one for helping or giving to others, as for birthday, Christmas, or for needy folks in the community; one for church offering; and one for his own spending money. The savings could be for some large useful item he needs in the near future or even for his college education. He should be encouraged to spend the part for himself on his projects or practical things. This might include wood and nails for carpentry, nature books, seeds, clothes, or equipment of lasting value, such as a sleeping bag.

Accumulating certain parts of his allowance for several weeks in order to buy something worthwhile will give the child valuable practice in management. He should never get into the habit of "borrowing" next week's allowance ahead of time or from the part set aside for something else. The young manager should have a notebook to keep account of his income—everything he receives—and his expenses—absolutely every cent he spends.

Alert parents can help their youngsters be enterprising. Even though children under sixteen often cannot have regular jobs, some children who have learned to work well and know the value of money seem to be able to find ways to earn what they need. We do not want to exalt money as a goal in itself or blow its worth out of proportion, but we believe economy and frugality combine with careful accounting to build integrity, thoughtfulness, and a more secure future. One child we know helps his mother take care of little children and shares in the income. In the spring, he had a garage sale. He built on this experience to go to a church bazaar where he sold popcorn and lemonade. He had a nice profit even after donating half to the church.

Most people are soft touches to buy from children who sell things, especially if they sell something which almost everyone can use. Good quality garden produce is largely profit if your child grows it himself. In some parts of the country, fruit and vegetable growers let people come in and buy wholesale what they pick for themselves. Your child could do this, then sell at a higher price to those who don't have time to pick, and retain the difference as pay for his work.

Living for Others

We feel strongly that children should have opportunities to help others who are not so fortunate as they. Service for those who need it helps to keep them from being self-centered and brings much satisfaction and pleasure. They will learn to be kind, considerate, and unselfish in their association with people as they follow your example and practice with you in your everyday manner of showing concern for others.

All children seem to outgrow most of their clothes before they wear them out. If the clothes have been properly cared for, others can use them. If your child has no brothers or sisters to wear his hand-me-downs, find another family who needs them, and let your child help pick out clothes to give. If not, take the clothes to a center where needy families are helped. Try to stay long enough for your child to watch how it is operated. He should be encouraged to share his earnings with the poor and with worthy community projects, and to share his tithe with his God.

If you have a garden, you will most likely have some produce you can give away. Be sure to involve your child in planning and distributing these gifts. Things you make together in the kitchen can be shared with others also.

If possible, take your child to visit a hospital, or a children's home on a regular basis.

One day we took Dennis and Kathie with us when we went to a hospital to see a mother who had some complications while giving birth. Since they could only look through the nursery window and soon tired, I took them over to the pediatric ward while Dorothy engaged in talk "between us girls." The first child we saw had suffered brain damage from a freak bicycle accident and the second had been injured in a motorcycle mishap. The need for caution was deeply impressed in our children, who were just developing a taste for these vehicles. We had gone to the hospital to give comfort. And this should be our high motive. But it seems that every time we also learned valuable practical lessons for ourselves.

Whether hospital, convalescent center, children's home, or other institution, let your child reach out to others.

Even if you are a single parent, your child has a great advantage over those who have no parent or relatives of any kind. Such experiences help him appreciate what he has. Let him make, buy, or share something he already has with a sick or crippled child. Some children's wards in hospitals can use scrapbooks and other toys that may be stuffing your child's closet.

Older folks are often in special need of cheering up and helping. If your family sings together, arrange to go and sing some songs for a shut-in person or for a convalescent home or retirement center. Managers of such facilities are usually glad for attention to these lonely people. You might even "adopt" an especially needy one for extra care and attention.

Don't forget younger children. Even the child's younger brother or sister often needs help or comfort. To help him learn how to put himself in another's place, perhaps he can remember what it was like to be little and not very competent. Such expectations should not be too demanding, but caring for each other is an important family responsibility.

Help your good Samaritan learn by precept and example the true meaning of the Golden Rule. This means we do not litter, misuse equipment in parks or other public facilities, or overuse the natural resources of our country because we have concern for others who have needs or who come after us. A seven-, eight-, or nine-year-old can learn to understand and practice these principles even though he constantly sees others who do not.

Teach him by both precept and example that unselfish concern for others also involves keeping our promises, returning things we have borrowed, and paying for anything we have damaged. Rudeness, thoughtlessness, even vandalism have become almost epidemic in our country because of our self-centered generation. This is a serious breakdown in society that you and your child can begin reversing first of all in your home.

Learning Principles: The Basic Whys

The growing ability to reason consistently brings another milestone in the area of self-government. Your child is now more able to talk things over and even to make reasonable compromises and "bargains." He can better understand the rights, motives, and viewpoints of others which until now have been out of his ken. We hope he has developed a rather strong sense of fairness and a conviction of what is right or wrong. This does not mean that he is always ready to stand up to the pressures of his peers in this respect, because his values may still not be firmly established. But it does mean that you must be alert to keep the promises you make and to be straightforward in your dealings with him and with others. He is particular about rules or laws of the home, of games, of your driving, or whatever he is involved in. He will probably notice any infractions.

If the first steps in discipline have been carefully followed, your seven-, eight- or nine-year-old should be making more and more of his own decisions, on the basis of principles—*the basic reasons why* he does things—as much as is practicable. He should have plenty of practice in thinking and acting for himself so that his judgment, like a muscle, will grow stronger with use. If you are consistent, he will also learn the wisdom of respecting your experienced counsel and judgment and that of other responsible adults.

The principles on which he makes his decisions are the family values that have been demonstrated and taught from babyhood by conversations and stories he has heard, experiences he has had, and models he has watched. He will continue to internalize such principles by the same methods. If your example has been sound and he has not been unduly affected by undesirable peer or other influences, his choices will usually be right. They involve his food, dress, manners, attitudes, amusements, morals, and physical habits. As a matter of fact, what he has learned in these early years has more to do with his basic character than all he learns in the future. The great Jesuit leader, Francis Xavier, said, "Give me the children until they are seven and anyone may have them afterwards."

When your child consults you about a problem or for permission for something, be sure you make use of the opportunity to help him make a decision. Try not to make it for him. Ask lots of questions rather than handing out advice. Such reasonableness will encourage him to counsel with you and produce a more cooperative spirit. Do not hesitate to take a strong stand if necessary. Children want and need parents who love them enough to care what they do. In the long run, they will respect you for your concern and consistency. A child who has achieved independent and internalized values by consistent parental example and training without interference from institutions will not so easily cave in to his peers just because "everybody is doing it." The parents, we repeat, not age-mates, are the child's best socializers, and, it is to be hoped, his best examples. They are the best purveyors of principle.

Thinking More to Live Better

Here is an experiment to illustrate the principle that whole wheat bread usually digests better and is more nutritious than white bread. Give your child a half slice of store-bought white bread and a half slice of *100 percent* whole wheat bread. Let him wad each piece into a ball. If it is of good quality the whole wheat bread will crumble, while the white bread will form a gummy ball. Talk about how it would be in the stomach and which the digestive juices could digest best. Secure a natural wheat stalk if possible and show your child how the outer bran and germ is taken out of the grain for white flour.

Tell about the experiments which have been conducted with one group of rats that ate whole wheat bread versus another group that ate white bread. Let him guess the result—that the rats who ate the white bread became sick and died. We believe that he will decide he prefers whole wheat bread.

One of the world's leading rice researchers, Dr. Kondo of Kyoto University, told us that the outer 15 percent of the grain that is normally refined away contains 98 percent of the vitamins and minerals. Teach your child by example to give his body the best food. Explain that every time the body takes in refined sugars and other foods—as in candy, soft drinks, sweet rolls, sugared cereals, free sugar—it must provide minerals to digest them. Ask him, if they are not in the foods themselves, where will they come from, except to rob his body? Help him to eat to live and not live to eat.

Another principle you may want to instill early is that alcohol is a dangerous drink because it makes a person lose control of his reason and his body and destroys the neurons or cells of his brain. Let him smell some alcohol beverage in contrast to orange juice so that he will notice that it doesn't even smell sweet and good. When you are walking, ask him to walk on a straight line. Then tell him that a person who drinks a few cocktails or beers cannot walk a straight line but veers from side to side. He could illustrate this on a paper with a house on one side and a store on the other. A straight line between would be the path of a man who does not drink while a wobbly line is the path of a man who drinks alcohol. You may also be able to show him a wrecked automobile which was caused by a drinking driver. Explain how such a driver cannot judge distances or drive safely. A decision never to drink even at this relatively early age can have far-reaching good results.

The dangers of smoking likewise should be taught both by

precept and example. Describe the many poisons, the darkened lungs and crippled body, the lack of self-control, and finally the hacking cough, cancer surgery, heart attack or choking to death that may result from smoking. Ask the child if he or she wants to be his own person or a slave to a drug. It is during these early years of reason that you can do much to build the child's habits for life.

The effect of health habits on the body makes more sense to him now than ever before. He can understand more clearly the importance of washing his hands before meals, after work or play, and after using the toilet; of brushing his teeth after meals and before going to bed; the necessity of good light when looking at a book or doing other close work. He can begin to comprehend what germs do and how they are spread; how diet affects our bodies, including our teeth and bones. Take advantage of his reasoning power to help him make decisions about the care of his body, and provide him with significant information that applies to him.

One of the common problems of young children is insufficient sleep. Your child should understand that he needs eleven to twelve hours of sleep and that short-changing the body requirements in this respect can have long-term effects. When he realizes that growth takes place and muscles, nerves, and energy are built up during sleep, he should be interested in doing what will be best for him. He also needs to know that the best quality of sleep occurs in the hours before midnight.

Since poor posture can easily develop at this age, help your child appreciate the value of sitting and standing correctly. Suggest that he pretend that he walks suspended from a string so that he will think of himself as tall and straight. Also let him practice walking while balancing a book on his head to develop a smooth, graceful walk. Help him understand that inadequate rest and sleep is a cause of poor posture.

School Just Ahead

There is logical progression in the early development of children. They do not achieve their abilities at the same age but there is a natural sequence each child follows. Infants babble before they talk; they usually creep before they walk, and so on.

Before a child can efficiently read books about the world he lives in, he must see, hear, smell, touch, and taste that world. If he has not built up a background of firsthand experience, he will not be as well equipped as he should be to make use of his natural ability and desire to learn. Your child's earliest learning is informal and intuitive without his having any particular understanding of what he is doing. It involves all phases of his life—physical, mental, and emotional—and includes language, motor skills, and certain social skills. The young child is extremely imitative, sensitive to his environment and receptive to whatever stimulation is available. The skills and impressions thus gained are of lifelong duration and form a basic mold for intellectual achievement later on.

If any of this basic learning has not been allowed to progress long enough before formal learning begins, the child will not grow in balance. It is quite possible to teach a bright three- or four-year-old to read, but while he is spending time doing that he is missing out on something more essential to that stage of his development—something he may not be able to make up later. Premature emphasis on any learning, particularly by rote memory, can close pathways to other learning. When leaders of student radicals were studied in the late '60s, it was found in most cases that intellect had been developed at too early an age with a corresponding lack in emotional development. These young adults had brilliant minds but had progressed emotionally only to the temper-tantrum stage.

Eight is the minimum fail-safe age for a child to enter school, but any delay up to that time is an advantage to the child over those who start at the traditional age of five or six. In other words, seven is better than six for first grade, and six is better than five for kindergarten. Bear in mind that many children, especially boys, may not be ready until nine or ten. They will not lose by delaying another year or two; rather, they will be better off by waiting. This does not mean that they might not be learning some school tasks at home, but this would normally be without pressure. Many children seem to teach themselves to read. You may even have to tactfully restrain some from putting too much time and attention on books.

Try to get them involved in other activities most of the time so that they will develop in balance.

Where to Start

One thing stands out as quite important once you decide your child is ready for school. *In most cases, he should start with his age-mates.* Having an older or larger child in with the first grade "babies" may embarrass him, and his graduation from high school should not be delayed to age twenty. All studies of early and late starters show that in general those who were older not only caught up with but surpassed the younger starters academically, socially, and behaviorally.

If your school has a non-graded primary room or similar flexible system, you are fortunate. Any reasonably well-trained teacher, flexible in her methods, can bring your child up to grade level, and perhaps beyond, by the end of the school year. He will learn in a few months what it took the others two or three years to learn. Only he will continue his excitement for learning when most of the others are getting tired or bored. First-graders traditionally regress considerably in their learning over the summer and have a lot of relearning to do in the second grade. The loss is not so great after the second grade but is noticeable nevertheless. If your child starts school in the third grade at age eight, for example, he will learn much faster and retain better than those who started at six, without the anxiety, frustration, or failure most early starters sadly know.

If you find that your school is rigid in insisting that every child must be tested first and then placed at his *achievement* level, we suggest a simple, short home program for the last six months or so before school starts. We are assuming, of course, that he is very near or over age eight and that he is average in maturity for his age. On a one-to-one basis you can accomplish more at home in an hour or two than it takes a teacher the whole day to do with a classroom of children. "Social studies" and elementary science should have been a part of your informal home program all along:

You have visited the firehouse, perhaps a bakery or other manufacturing process and have become acquainted with community activities. You have learned about weather, animals, birds, and other natural phenomena. You have been reading to your child twenty or thirty minutes a day, and he has counted and measured many things with you.

So reading, writing, spelling, arithmetic, and language skills are all you have to work on. Workbooks are usually available inexpensively for these subjects, and will give you everything you need except for the readers. When possible, you may want to obtain the same series as the school you expect your child to attend. A list of excellent sources is included at the close of this book in Appendix 1.

Yet we stress that even this special study is not necessary if your child's first teacher—in the second, third or fourth grade—is a person who understands how children develop and who practices two basic principles of teaching. These are, first, start the pupil at his achievement level, and, second, proceed at his rate. Chances are your child will be ahead in some things—including practical experience—and can be used to help other children. The wise teacher will also use others to help your child where he may be slow. But it is likely that he will catch up and even pass many of his classmates before the end of the school year.

You have carefully monitored your child's health. He has had regular checkups by a qualified physician, and any physical defects or problems have long ago been treated or corrected insofar as possible. If your child is handicapped, you have sought and received specialized help in training him. The most recent trend even for such unusual children is for parents to be more involved in their education, with help and instruction from specialists in the particular field of need. However, you should make sure that a very thorough physical examination is done for your child well before school entry. This should include a careful check on his vision and hearing. Too often, preventable difficulties are discovered only after a troubled, unsuccessful, and unhappy year or more in school.

If you have already sent your child to school too early and he is bored or misbehaving, there is still much that you usually can do to help him. Three principles are vital here. They are parental warmth, physical work, and service for others: (1) Respond warmly and consistently to your child, so that he feels needed and depended upon. (2) Work with him in the home and yard, teaching him responsibility, industry, neatness, dependability, and self-control. (3) Help him to understand and appreciate the rewards of doing things for others, including his family; for the young and old; for the sick and poor or less fortunate. There is no more certain pathway to self-worth than these, no personality and character remedy so sure.

By popular request this edition includes the friendly "Moore Formula," homeschooling's most proven curriculum for parents and children as well as many creative classroom teachers.

THE MOORE FORMULA

*Note: Raymond and Dorothy Moore are professionals known around the world, he for reorganizing colleges and universities and for establishing highly-successful work-study programs; she as a world-class curriculum and reading authority, and both as child specialists who shared in the founding of modern homeschooling. The Moore Formula uses methods proven by thousands of the world's most successful families and schools to help parents who want high character, achievement and sociability. With over 300 research associates, Moores report studies world-wide in journals and books including the media and 1) their books **Better Late Than Early (BLTE), and School Can Wait (SCW),** and 2) highly successful methods for parents in **The Successful Home School Family Handbook** (update of **Home School Burnout**) **(The Handbook)** and **Minding Your Own Business (MYOB).** For low-cost, low stress curricula and how to be a Moore Foundation Associate (MFA), send a self-addressed, stamped envelope to Box 1, Camas WA 98607.*

Reality
If you doubt student or teacher burnout or your own ability, join any Moore seminar or read *The Handbook.* It's not mostly from intellectual or spiritual problems, as some suggest, but from wrong habit or method. We help you avoid or cure fear, frustration, boredom, stress, pain, despair, heavy expense. Teaching should be mostly fun: relaxing, healing, inexpensive, low-stress yet successful like Tom Edison, Abe Lincoln and Christ.

A Better Way
After 55 years of teaching teachers and students and managing education at all levels, we give you here and in *The Handbook* secrets of the ages to avoid or cure burnout and failure, to bring success beyond normal hopes. To our knowledge, we have no failures! Even drill can be fun. Allow for individual differences, follow the principled and balanced Moore Formula, and your normal children will excel in head, hand, heart, and health, proven as it is by history, research and common sense.

The Formula
1. **Study** from a few minutes to several hours per day, depending on the child's maturity.
2. **Manual work** *at least* as much as study.
3. **Home and/or community service** an hour or so a day. Focus on kid's interests and needs; be an example in consistency, curiosity and patience. **Live with them!** Worry less about tests; we'll help you there. **With the Moore Formula, if you are loving and can read, write, count, and speak clearly, you are a master teacher.**

STUDY	WORK	SERVICE
30" to 180" Daily	*30" to 180" Daily*	*Variable Times*
Warm responsive parents who know their children's interests. Drill to develop their phonics, writing, and math when the children are ready in senses, brain and reasoning.	Children combine household chores (from the time they learn to walk) with home industries in which they share management. They learn math, etc. by earning money and accounting for it.	Service begins at home and in the neighborhood, with daily or weekly visits to nursing homes, pediatric wards or other ventures in community or personal service.
Encourage them to freely explore their ideas with few restrictions by workbooks and school methods, reaching out as interests expand.	They also become well and positively socialized as they buy and sell. And they build character as they work and serve.	*Note: The time you devote to study work or service should depend upon the children's maturity and interests. Teens are easiest of all with Moore's Formula.*

Study
Moores' free exploring curricula are largely self-teaching: Math-it, Winston Grammar, etc. Use fewer workbooks and textbooks. Generally parents are the best teachers for their children. The Smithsonian Institution's study of twenty world-class geniuses stressed three factors:
1. Warm, loving, educationally responsive parents and other adults.
2. Scant association outside the family.
3. A great deal of creative freedom under **parental guidance** to explore their ideas, drilling as necessary.
These ingredients for genius are a mixture of head, hand, heart and health—a neat fit into the chart above. Mixed in balance, with **your sound example**, they bring out great characters and personalities. So we encourage you to unite 1) study, 2) work (and entrepreneurship) with 3) home and community service:

224

How To Begin

First, don't subject your children to formal, scheduled study before the age 8 to 10 or 12, whether they can read or not. To any who differ, ask their evidence. Let them read *BLTE* or *SCW*. In addition to our basic research at Stanford and the University of Colorado Medical School, we analyzed over 8000 studies of children's senses, brain, cognition, socialization, etc., and are certain that **no replicable evidence exists for rushing children into formal study** *at home or school* **before 8 to 10.**

Read, sing and play with your children from birth. Read to them several times a day, and they will learn to read in their own time–as early as 3 or 4, but usually later, some as late as 14. Late readers are no more likely to be retarded or disabled than early ones. They often become the best readers of all–with undamaged vision and acute hearing, more adult-like reasoning (cognition) levels, mature brain structure less blocking of creative interests. Yet late readers are often falsely thought to be in need of remedial help. If you have any doubts about your youngsters, have specialists check vision and hearing; possibly see a neurologist; if there are no problems, relax.

If your children are early readers, 15 or 20 minutes at a time is enough for children under 8 or 10. They can use a kitchen timer. Then take an hour or two for distant vision play. They can first use crayons or chalk on large paper or blackboards before developing finer muscle coordination required for pencils or detailed drawing or sewing. More on this in *BLTE, SCW* and *Home Grown Kids*.

When your children seem ready, play oral games with phonics, numbers, etc., but authorities from Columbia to Cal-Berkeley say avoid study pressures until they are at least 8 to 12. At that time a few minutes a day may be all that is necessary for the drill or practice in basics they need. Just as important–or more so–is to identify their interests such as bugs, gardening, cooking or baking, astronomy, cars, sewing, cottage industries, economics, history or politics.

Whatever their interests, open the door wide to knowledge. Don't give them mostly text/work books nor try to keep ahead of them; let them do original reading along the lines of their interests and watch them grow! A child's motivation is more educationally productive than fanciest teaching. And let them sample old standardized tests or manuals to lose the fear of testing.

Instead of toys, give them tools (kitchen, shop, yard or desk), encyclopedias, magazines; use libraries, etc. Don't be shocked at their interests, even if they are guns or motorcycles! From these they can learn chemistry and physics (internal combustion motors), economics, math, history, geography, languages, cultures and manual skills (at local repair shops or in home businesses). Girls are usually a year or so ahead of boys.

The "antennae" sprouting from the brains of most students are blocked by mass-education's cookie-cutter substitutes for life that destroy creativity. Kids come out uniform-sized cookies or sausages. Better to learn history realistically by reading biographies rather than textbooks. Let creative interests expand to other learning. As they mature, they teach themselves, learn at their own initiative–as few now do!

Work
Constructive, skill-building, entrepreneurial work builds childrens' self-control, and does it more quickly. It is the most dramatic and consistent cure for behavior and personality problems, If you give children authority to manage your home to the extent that they can accept responsibility, they mature rapidly and naturally. Make them officers in your home industries. **There is no more certain key to happy home education–or other schooling–regardless of institutional level. We've seen no one fail, rebel, or burnout.**

Begin small. Start your children to work when they start to walk. Add freedom as they accept responsibility. No cash allowances! Let them earn their way, helping you make or grow and sell cookies, muffins, bread, wooden toys, vegetables, or service lawns, baby-sit, etc. By 6 or 8, many can run businesses. See *MYOB* for more than 400 cottage industries. Do comparison shopping: apples/oranges, Grapenuts/sugar pops, etc. (nutrition, frugality and math lessons). Let your kids use your checking account to pay your bills. The bank corrects their "papers."

Service
This begins at home and neighborhood with daily/weekly visits to needy neighbors, nursing homes, pediatric wards or other community or personal service. It makes self-centered kids self-less and moderates any tendency their businesses bring toward materialism. Family, community and church provide fruitful ways of building great-hearted children. Some *schools* now use service as a wholesome activity. Children who are too young to be allowed to visit in pediatric wards are usually welcomed in nursing homes with bouquets of wild flowers or crayon drawings.

This is the golden rule in practice. Our children once had a secret society ("SOS" –for Service Over Self) that specialized in secret good deeds for the aged, poor, sick, or handicapped–like washing or repairing a car or chair or washing machine, or painting fences, shoveling snow or weeding gardens. Great fun! Often they told the police in advance lest they be arrested for "trespassing."

Some ask why more families don't follow this formula. Most parents are uncomfortable with unconventional ideas. They teach as they were taught, unaware that such methods are responsible for many of today's school problems. So they pay heavily for books which tie them and their children down and burn them out. To them we as professionals say, "It took us a while to believe too." Certified teachers often have the hardest times. Moore students average near the top in student achievement, sociability, and behavior and at low stress and cost. Carefully read *The Successful Home School Family Handbook (update of Home School Burnout)* and *Minding Your Own Business*, then *Home Made Health, Home Built Discipline* and *Better Late Than Early*. You will have both security and joy!

Gentle Warning: **Properly done, home education offers low stress, low cost, and high achievement and sociability from a balance of study, work, and service. Few curricula do this!** Insist on proven research and experience. Patiently study methods and materials before you send your check and credit card number to anyone. Question closely *all* testers, lecturers and entrepreneurs. Insist they prove their quality. Home school leaders like those in pro-life and anti-porn fall into two groups: 1) Selfless laymen and professionals and officials who sacrifice money and time to elevate homeschooling to new heights; and 2) A few lacking professional background or ethics or both, who urge *stressful, costly* school-at-home materials, programs or services on unwary parents who then burn out and come to loathe homeschool. Some *fought* home-schooling until the 1980's. Some authors, editors and speakers know little of research, and persuasively misuse Scripture to convey an image of a bigoted Christ to secular friends. They are homeschools' most divisive influence. For your sake and for your friends', study to know the difference.

In summary, after you look at all the other curricula, examine the original: Homeschool's non-profit, low-stress, researched-based, high-achievement Moore Formula from the Moore Academy, pioneers of the modern homeschool movement.

The Moore Foundation Staff
Box 1, Camas, WA 98607
(206) 835-2736

REFERENCES AND RESOURCES

1. Ames, Louise B. *Is Your Child in the Wrong Grade?* New York: Harper & Row, 1967.
2. ———. *Stop School Failure.* New York: Harper & Row, 1972.
3. Ames, Louise B. and Chase, J. A. *Don't Push Your Preschooler.* New York: Harper & Row, 1974.
4. Atkin, J. Myron. In *Time,* 16 June 1980, p. 54.
5. Bayley, Nancy. "Development of Mental Abilities." *Carmichael's Manual of Child Psychology,* vol. 1. John Mussen, ed. New York: Wiley & Sons, pp. 1163–1209, 1970.
6. Bloom, Benjamin S. *Stability and Change in Human Characteristics.* New York: Wiley & Sons, 1964.
7. Bowlby, John. *Attachment and Loss,* vol. 11, "Separation: Anxiety and Anger." New York: Basic Books, 1973.
8. Brackbill, Yvonne, et al. "Psychophysiologic Effects in the Neonate of Prone Versus Supine Placement," *Journal of Pediatrics* 82: 82–84, January 1973.
9. Bradley, Robert A. *Husband-Coached Childbirth.* New York: Harper and Row, 1974.
10. Brazelton, T. Barry, "What Childbirth Drugs Can Do to Your Child," *Redbook,* February 1971, p. 65.
11. Brenner, A. and Stott, L. H. "School Readiness Factor Analyzed." Detroit: Merrill-Palmer Institute, 1973.
12. Bronfenbrenner, Urie. "The American Family, Who Cares." A film series. Films obtainable from Institute for Family Studies. Cornell University, Ithaca, NY 14850.
13. ———. "The Social Ecology of Human Development." In *Brain and Intelligence: The Ecology of Child Development,* ed. Frederick Richardson. Hyattsville, MD: National Educational Press, 1973.

14. ———. *Two Worlds of Childhood: U.S. and U.S.S.R.* New York: Simon and Schuster, 1970.

15. Coopersmith, S. *The Antecedents of Self-Esteem.* San Francisco: W. H. Freeman & Co., 1967.

16. Douglass, Malcolm P. "Innovation and Credibility Gap." Address to California Elementary School Administrators Association and the California Association for Supervision and Curriculum Development, Palo Alto, 19 January 1968.

17. Elkind, David. "The Case for the Academic Preschool: Fact or Fiction?" *Young Children* 25 (January 1970).

18. ———. "Piagetian and Psychometric Conceptions of Intelligence." *Harvard Educational Review* 39 (Spring 1969): 319–37.

19. Engel, Martin. "Rapunzel, Rapunzel, Let Down Your Golden Hair: Some Thoughts on Early Childhood Education." Unpublished manuscript, National Demonstration Center in Early Childhood Education, U. S. Office of Education, Washington, D.C.

20. Feshbach, N. "Student Teacher Preferences for Elementary School Pupils Varying in Personality Characteristics." *Journal of Educational Psychology* 60: 126–32.

21. Fisher, James T. and Lowell S. Hawley. *A Few Buttons Missing.* Philadelphia: Lippincott, 1951.

22. Forester, John J. "At What Age Should a Child Start School?" *The School Executive*, March 1955, pp. 80–81.

23. Forgione, P. D. and Moore, R. S. "The Rationales for Early Childhood Education Policy Making." Prepared for the U.S. Office of Economic Opportunity under Research Grant No. 50079–G–73/01.

24. Formaneck, R. and Woog, P. "Attitudes of Preschool and Elementary School Children to Authority Figures." *Child Study Journal* 1: 100–110.

25. Geber, Marcelle. "The Psycho-Motor Development of African Children in the First Year, and the Influence of Maternal Behavior." *Journal of Social Psychology* 47 (1958): 185–95.

26. Gesell, Arnold and Ilg, Frances L. *The Child from Five to Ten.* New York: Harper and Bros., 1946.

27. Gesell, Arnold. *The Normal Child and Primary Education.* New York: Ginn & Co., 1912.

28. ———. "Pestalozzi and the Parent-Child Relationship," Reprinted from the *Amerikanische Schweizer Zeitung,* 9 October 1946.

29. Hilgartner, Henry L. "The Frequency of Myopia in Individuals under

21 Years of Age." Paper presented to the Texas Medical Society, Austin, Texas, 1962.

30. Jencks, Christopher S. "The Coleman Report and the Conventional Wisdom." *On Equality of Educational Opportunity.* Frederick Mosteller and Daniel P. Moynihan, eds. New York: Random House, 1972, pp. 37–42.

31. Jensen, Arthur R. "How Much Can We Boost IQ and Scholastic Achievement?" *Harvard Educational Review* 39 (1969): 1–123.

32. Keniston, Kenneth. *All Our Children: The American Family Under Pressure.* Carnegie Council on Children. New York: Harcourt Brace Jovanovich, 1977.

33. Klaus, Marshall, et al. "Maternal Attachment: Importance of the First Post-Partum Days," *New England Journal of Medicine* 286 (2 March 1972): 460–63.

34. Lamaze, Fernand. *Painless Childbirth,* Chicago: H. Regnery Co., 1970.

35. Lasch, Christopher. *The Culture of Narcissism.* New York: W. W. Norton, 1978.

36. Leboyer, Frederick. *Birth Without Violence.* New York: Knopf, 1975.

37. *Liberty* Magazine, Washington, DC 20012. November/December, 1979. Used by permission.

38. Ludlam, W. "Young Readers May Harm Eyes." *South Bend* (Indiana) *Tribune,* 12 December 1974, p. 34.

39. Metcalf, D. R. "An Investigation of Cerebral Lateral Functioning and the EEG." Report of a study made for the U. S. Office of Economic Opportunity, 1975.

40. Moon, R. D. and Moore, R. S. "The Effect of Early School Entrance on the School Achievement and Attitudes of Disadvantaged Children." Report of a study made for the U.S. Office of Economic Opportunity, 1975.

41. Moore, Raymond S. and Dorothy N. Moore. *Better Late Than Early.* New York: Reader's Digest–McGraw Hill, 1976, pp. 100–105.

42. Moore, Raymond S. *China Doctor.* New York: Harper & Row, 1961.

43. Moore, Raymond, et al. *School Can Wait.* Utah: Brigham Young University Press, 1979.

44. Moore, R. S., Moon, R. D. and Moore, D. R. "The California Report: Early Schooling for All?" *Phi Delta Kappan* 53 (1972): 615–21.

45. Newton, F. H. Letter to R. S. Moore, October 24, 1972.

46. Ortega y Gasset, Jose. *The Revolt of the Masses.* New York: W. W. Norton & Company, Inc., 1932.
47. Perry, James. *Wall Street Journal,* November 2, 1978.
48. Piaget, J. "Development and Learning." *Journal of Research in Science Teaching* 2 (1964): 176–86.
49. ———. "The Genetic Approach to the Psychology of Thought." *Journal of Educational Psychology* 52 (1961): 275–81.
50. ———. *The Origins of Intelligence in Children* (trans. M. Cook). New York: International Universities Press, 1952.
51. ———. *Science of Education and the Psychology of the Child.* New York: Viking Press, 1970.
52. Robinson, Meredith L. "Compensatory Education and Early Adolescence." Unpublished manuscript. Stanford Research Institute, 1973.
53. Rohwer, William D., Jr. in *Today's Child,* 20 May 1972.
54. Shannon, William V. "A Radical Direct, Simple, Utopia Alternative to Day-Care Centers." *New York Times,* 30 April 1972.
55. Skeels, Harold M. "Adult Status of Children with Contrasting Early Life Experiences, A Follow-up Study." Monograph of the Society for Research in Child Development. Chicago: University of Chicago Press, 1966.
56. ———, et al. *A Study of Environmental Stimulation: An Orphanage Preschool Project.* University of Iowa Studies in Child Welfare, vol. 15, no. 4. Iowa City, IA: University of Iowa Press, 1938.
57. *Time,* 26 July 1971, p. 38. "Getting Smarter Sooner."
58. U.S. Supreme Court: Farmington v. Tokushige 273 U.S. 284 (1927).
59. ———: Fowler v. Rhode Island 345 U.S. 67 (1953).
60. ———: Welsh v. United States 398 U.S. 333 (1970); United States v. Seeger 380 U.S. 163, 166 (1965), etc.
61. ———: Wisconsin v. Yoder 406 U.S. 205 (1972); Griswold v. Connecticut 381 U.S. 479 (1965); Pierce v. Society of Sisters 268 U.S. 510 (1925), etc.
62. Weaver, Gerald N. "A Study to Determine the Approximate Age Level Most Effective for Initiating the Study of Violin." *Lyons Music News* 13 (November 1967).
63. Wepman, Joseph M. "The Modality Concept—Including a Statement of the Perceptual and Conceptual Levels of Learning." *Perception and Reading,* Proceedings of the Twelfth Annual Con-

vention, International Reading Association, Newark, Delaware, 1968, pp. 1–6.

64. Wood, Camilla S., Brigham Young University, Provo, Utah. Letter to R. S. Moore, November 13, 1980.

65. Young, Francis A., et al. "The Transmission of Refractive Errors within Eskimo Families." *American Journal of Optometry and Archives of American Academy of Optometry* 46 (1969): 676–85.